James & Whitehead
on Life after Death

James & Whitehead on Life after Death

David Ray Griffin

ANOKA, MINNESOTA 2022

James and Whitehead on Life after Death

© 2022 Process Century Press

All rights reserved. Except for brief quotations in critical publications and reviews, no part of this book may be reproduced in any manner without prior permission from the publisher.

Process Century Press
RiverHouse LLC
802 River Lane
Anoka, MN 55303

Process Century Press books are published in association with the International Process Network.

Cover: Susanna Mennicke

VOLUME: IX
THEOLOGICAL EXPLORATIONS
JEANYNE B. SLETTOM, GENERAL EDITOR

ISBN 978-1-940447-52-0
Printed in the United States of America

SERIES PREFACE: THEOLOGICAL EXPLORATIONS

This series aims to explore the implications of Whiteheadian philosophy and theology for religious belief and practice. It also proposes that process religious thinkers, working from within many different traditions—Buddhist, Confucian, Christian, Hindu, Indigenous, Jewish, Muslim, and others—have unique insights pertinent to the critical issues of our day.

In 1976, we published a book, *Process Theology: An Introductory Exposition,* in which we aimed to "show the creative potentiality of a process perspective in theology." In addition to its explanation of process concepts and their application to Christian doctrine, the book noted the contribution of Whiteheadian thought toward "intercultural and interreligious understanding" and took an early stance on the ecological threat, claiming that process theology was prepared to "make a distinctive contribution" to this challenge.

Since the publication of that book, we have seen many others explore these and other themes in articles, books, and conferences. At the same time, the threat to planetary health and the need for "intercultural and interreligious understanding" has only accelerated. This series is an effort to support theologians and religious philosophers in their ongoing exposition of possible Whiteheadian solutions.

John B. Cobb, Jr.
David Ray Griffin

OTHER BOOKS IN THIS SERIES

God of Empowering Love, David P. Polk
God Exists but Gawd Does Not, David Ray Griffin
Counter-Imperial Churching for a Planetary Gospel, Timothy Murphy
Process Theology, David Ray Griffin
The Christian Gospel for Americans, David Ray Griffin
Salvation, John B. Cobb, Jr.
Reinhold Niebuhr & the Question of Global Democracy, David Ray Griffin
What Is Process Thought? Seven Answers to Seven Questions, Jay McDaniel

Contents

Preface, i

Introduction, 1

1. The Importance of Life after Death, 5
2. The Case against Life after Death, 17
3. Bacteria and the Mind-Body Problem, 19
4. Panpsychism or Panexperientialism, 25
5. James, Whitehead, and Psychical Research, 31
6. Mrs. Piper and Other Mediums, 53
7. Near-Death Out-of-Body Experiences, 69
8. Apparitions, 87
9. Reincarnation, 99
10. Why Human Souls May Alone Survive Death, 117
11. Our Fine-Tuned Universe and Panentheism, 125
12. Whitehead and James on the Question of Life after Death, 147

Conclusion, 155

Appendix I: Jamesian-Whiteheadian Philosophy as Postmodern, 165

Appendix II: Panexperientialism Compared with Dualism and Materialism, 169

Dedication

For my wife, Ann Jaqua, and my daughter, Lydia Beth

Preface

THERE HAVE BEEN DOZENS OF BOOKS advocating life after death. But most of them do not provide fully convincing evidence for this belief. There are various reasons why they fail.

First, some of these books appeal to divine revelation provided by religious scriptures, be they Christian, Islamic, Hindu, or something else. As such, they do not provide evidence for people who do not accept these scriptures. The present book does not presuppose revelation from a particular religious tradition.

Second, some of these books do appeal to evidence that in principle can by accepted by anyone, such as evidence provided by psychical research. However, the evidence is typically presented within a worldview that is not shown to be self-consistent and adequate to the facts of experience. The present book differs by virtue of looking at the evidence within the framework of two of our major English-speaking philosophers, William James and Alfred North Whitehead, who were especially concerned to deal with all types of experience (see the comments by Edward Kelly in Chapter 5).

Third, these books often fail to deal critically with controversial claims typically involved in defenses of life after death. For example, they usually, seeing that a materialist worldview does not allow for life after death,[1] affirm mind-body dualism. But they typically do not deal with the problems that have led most recent philosophers to reject dualism as incoherent.

Fourth, it is generally assumed that life after death presupposes the existence of a divine reality, be it called "God," "Allah," or "Saguna Brahman." But most such books do not provide persuasive evidence for a divine reality. This book points to such evidence by reference to my 2016 book, *God Exists but Gawd Does Not: From Evil to New Atheism to Fine-Tuning*.[2] Chapter 11 of the present book provides one part of its evidence, which can serve as a stand-alone argument for the existence of a divine creator.

Endnotes

1. A few philosophers claim that materialism is compatible with belief in life after death; for example, Dean Zimmerman, "The Compatibility of Materialism and Survival: The 'Falling Elevator' Model" (*Faith and Philosophy: Journal of the Society of Christian Philosophers* 16.2 [April 1999]). But that belief presupposes divine omnipotence, and I find that to be a nonstarter.
2. *God Exists but Gawd Does Not: From Evil to New Atheism to Fine-Tuning* (Anoka, MN: Process Century Press, 2016).

Introduction

Philosopher Martin Heidegger said that a human being can be described as being-toward-death. The members of all species of living beings, of course, die. But we human beings are unique by virtue of anticipating our deaths.

There is nothing special about my anticipation of my own death. Rather, I am simply one of billions of living beings who have anticipated their own deaths. However, my death, along with that of other people in recent and subsequent decades, is unique in one respect: We have good evidence (although not proof) that our individual deaths may soon be followed by the death of our species as a whole. This fact makes our anticipations of our deaths unique. It may be that imminent extinction is humanity's fate.

In 2014, *New Yorker* writer Elizabeth Kolbert published a book entitled *The Sixth Extinction*. The title alludes to the fact that between 444 million and 66 million years ago, there were five mass extinctions, and we are now in the midst of the sixth. Kolbert asked: "In an extinction event of our own making, what happens to us?" Many people, she observed, seem to think that we self-named *Homo sapiens* are so wise and powerful that nothing could drive us to extinction. However, she pointed out, "When a mass extinction occurs, it takes out the weak and also lays low the strong."[1]

An organization called Extinction Rebellion said in 2018: "Based on the science, we have ten years at the most to reduce CO_2 emissions to zero, or the human race and most other species are at high risk of extinction within decades.[2] This estimation may be wrong; but it illustrates the fact that the issue is now discussed.

Australian microbiologist Frank Fenner, who had announced the eradication of smallpox in 1980, said in 2010 that *Homo sapiens* will become extinct, perhaps within 100 years.[3]

Guy R. McPherson, professor emeritus of evolutionary biology at the University of Arizona, has presented an array of scenarios through which humanity could become extinct in the near future, perhaps the most serious being methane emissions from thawing permafrost.[4]

The prediction of human extinction through methane emissions has been central to the thinking of retired Earth-systems scientist Malcolm Light, who wrote that methane release, which began in 2010, "will accelerate exponentially, release huge quantities of methane into the atmosphere and lead to the demise of all life on earth before the middle of this century."[5]

In August 2021, the United Nation's IPCC (Intergovernmental Panel on Climate Change) issued a report that the UN secretary general called "a code red for humanity."[6] A story about the report said: "if we were to substantially slash emissions in the next few years we could avoid the collapse of civilization"[7]—which seems to imply that, if we do not reduce them, civilization will not be saved.

In November of 2021, Dexter Wollersheim of Job One for Humanity wrote: "With the failure of COP26 Glasgow climate conference, we have entered into the era of Mutually Assured Climate Extinction (aka MACE)."[8]

Given this situation, some people find it difficult to maintain long-term hope of any kind, failing belief that an omnipotent deity will protect them from climate (as well as nuclear) holocaust, an idea for which there is no good evidence. Such people find it impossible to escape from the nihilistic hopelessness that would probably follow from the impending death of our planet, in the sense that it could no longer support advanced forms of life. But they could conclude that our fates would personally not be completely bleak, if they could see good reason to believe that human life continues after the death of our bodies.

It is true that some conservative-to-fundamentalist Christians are indifferent about the impending death of our planet, especially those who anticipate being caught up in a "rapture." I completely repudiate this theology and, more generally, this attitude about the death of Earth. If our planet dies, in the sense that it can no longer support higher forms of life, especially human beings, this will be the greatest tragedy in the universe or, if there are deaths of other planets with humanlike beings, one of the greatest tragedies. For people to anticipate life after bodily death in no way implies a devaluation of the importance of continued life in this world. But it will be a way of saying that our planet, whenever it occurs, will have made a permanent contribution to the universe.

This book will likely be most persuasive to people who, on the one hand, reject divine omnipotence and, on the other hand, are uncertain that the late modern worldview is the final truth about life and the universe. The book is also for people who, in William James's terms, are more concerned with discovering truth than avoiding error.

Chapter 1 discusses why the issue of life after death is important, especially today. Chapter 2 lays out the case against the idea of life after death.

Chapters 3–12 lay out a new, postmodern worldview, based significantly on the thought of William James and Alfred North Whitehead (on the use of the term "postmodern," see Appendix I: Jamesian-Whiteheadian Philosophy as Postmodern), which makes the idea of life after death seem less outrageous than it has recently seemed to most intellectuals.

Chapter 3 shows how microbiology has shown how the mind-body problem, which has been the most intractable philosophical problem since the seventeenth century, can be overcome.

Chapter 4 and Appendix II explain how the doctrine known as "panpsychism" or "panexperientialism," affirmed by both James and Whitehead, explains the mind-body relation better than do dualism and materialism, and in a way that allows for life after death.

Chapter 5 discusses psychical research and how Whitehead and James supported it.

Chapters 6–9 look at four types of experience-based evidence for life after death, which can be considered serious if, and only if, the reported experiences are corroborated.

Chapter 10 explains why, if humans do survive death, we may be the only species on our planet to do so.

Chapter 11 explains how the recent discovery of the fine-tuning of our universe makes belief in a divine creator virtually necessary—a belief that makes life after death more likely than does atheism. This chapter also explains how the doctrine called "panentheism" removes the standard objections to a divine creator.

Chapter 12 discusses the beliefs of James and Whitehead about life after death.

The conclusion summarizes the evidence for life after death in the context of the new worldview inspired by James, Whitehead, and psychical research.

Endnotes

1   Elizabeth Kolbert, *The Sixth Extinction: An Unnatural History* (New York: Henry Holt, 2014), 267–68.

2   Quoted in Dahr Jamail, "The Global Extinction Rebellion Begins," Truthout, 15 November 2018, https://truthout.org/articles/the-global-extinction-rebellion-begins/.

3   Lin Edwards, "Humans Will Be Extinct in 100 Years Says Eminent Scientist," Phys.org, 23 June 2010, https://phys.org/news/2010-06-humans-extinct-years-eminent-scientist.html.

4   Guy R. McPherson, "Three Paths to Near-term Human Extinction," Canadians for Emergency Action on Climate Change, 9 November 2011; "19 Ways Climate Change Is Now Feeding Itself," Transition Voice, 19 August 2013; *Going Dark* (Baltimore: PublishAmerica, 2013).

5   Malcolm Light, "Global Extinction within one Human Lifetime as a Result of a Spreading Atmospheric Arctic Methane Heat Wave and Surface Firestorm," Arctic News, 9 February 2012, https://arctic-news.blogspot.com/p/global-extinction-within-one-human.html.

6   Fiona Harvey, "Major Climate Changes Inevitable and Irreversible—IPCC's Starkest Warning Yet," *The Guardian,* 9 August 2021.

7   Richard Matthews, "IPCC Report Is Our Final Warning," The Green Market Oracle, 17 August 2021.

8   Dexter Wollersheim, Facing All the Facts, Job One for Humanity, November 23, 2021.

CHAPTER ONE

The Importance of Life after Death

In the world's various religions, the doctrine of human destiny has usually involved some mode of existence beyond bodily death. On the one hand, it has widely been held that, if some of the uniquely human problems are to be resolved, such a resolution could occur only in a life after death. On the other hand, some of the distinctively human capacities suggest that human beings might uniquely be capable of such a mode of existence, at least with divine assistance. In theistic religions, this expectation has been central to the belief in God as the ground of hope. This chapter looks at this issue from the point of view of Whiteheadian process philosophy.

The Anticipation of Death

The distinctive nature of human consciousness, with its element of self-consciousness, makes death a special problem for human beings. Besides the fact that we, like all other animals, will die sooner or later, we can consciously anticipate this fact. The usual assumption that this anticipation is unique to us on this planet is probably correct, at least largely. Even if some of the other higher animals have an inchoate anticipation of their own deaths, we appear to be the only ones with elaborate rituals and meaning-systems connected with death. In any case, because we do anticipate our own death and that of others, death is a problem, which seems to have at least four distinguishable dimensions.

1. *Ultimate Meaning*: First, our awareness that we will die raises the question whether our lives have any ultimate meaning. "Rational life," wrote Whitehead, "refuses to conceive itself as a transient enjoyment, transiently useful."[1] The problem can be stated in this way: if we believe we make no permanent contribution—that our lives are merely "transiently useful" at best—the resulting disappointment can empty our "transient enjoyment" of most of its enjoyment. Such a result would mean the evolutionary process had brought about a self-defeating result.

The purpose behind the evolutionary process is, by hypothesis, the development of creatures with increasingly greater capacity for intrinsic value. Human beings appear to be the apex of this development on our planet. And yet human existence, by virtue of its capacity to ask the question of ultimate meaning, can end up being less, rather than more, enjoyable than the other forms of animal existence. This sense of meaningless can lead to suicide.

We are aware that we will have a more or less extensive "social immortality," living on, in a sense, through the memory of others, through our descendants and through other contributions we may have made to human society. But we also know that memory fades and that, for most of us anyway, our contributions will become less and less significant as time passes. If we really reflect on this issue, furthermore, we are aware that the human race itself will eventually perish, so that so-called social immortality provides no real immortality at all. The resulting suggestion that our lives make no permanent contribution to anything, so that the universe will eventually be as if we had never been, raises the question of the meaning of our lives in the strongest possible terms.

We may have struggled mightily to realize certain aims, but reflection upon the impermanence of all finite structures raises the question whether our struggles really made any ultimate difference. Charles Hartshorne, who was Whitehead's assistant at Harvard and became the second major process philosopher after Whitehead, wrote:

Be the aim Nirvana, the Classless Society, the Welfare State, Self-realization, the query is never silenced, what good is it, from the cosmic and everlasting perspective, that one or the other or all of these aims be attained for a time on this ball of rock?[2]

If we give a nihilistic answer—that it makes no ultimate difference—this answer raises, in turn, the question of the reality of God, insofar as it belongs to the very idea of God to be the ultimate ground of the meaning of life. The nihilistic idea that life is meaningless, therefore, is closely connected to the idea that there is no Holy Reality. And that conclusion undermines the premise from which we started, that the evolutionary process is the expression of a cosmic purpose to realize value. Nihilism becomes total.

2. *Ultimate Justice*: A second dimension of the problem created by our awareness that we all die is that of ultimate justice. We are aware that human life is terribly unfair, that some people, through no merit of their own, are extremely fortunate, whereas others, through no fault of their own, are extremely unfortunate. Many are, for example, born into situations of abject poverty, from which there is no escape, or with terrible physical or mental deformities. Many others are born with great potential, but die young, before having had much chance to develop their potential.

Beyond these obvious facts, there is also the problem, emphasized by eighteenth-century philosopher Immanuel Kant, that a gap between virtue and happiness often exists, with immoral people often having happier lives than truly good people. The resulting intellectual problem, as Kant pointed out, is that these discrepancies throw into doubt the validity of our sense that there is a moral order to the universe. That is, the universe seems to call us to be moral (most of the religions of the world agree, Whitehead pointed out, on the "essential rightness of things"[3]). But if the universe itself is not just, then our confidence that it really contains objective moral principles is undermined, with the result that we are led toward moral nihilism. Kant believed that we could prevent this undermining only by postulating a life after death in which the gap between virtue and happiness would be progressively overcome.[4]

3. *Longing for More Life*: A third dimension of the problem raised by our anticipation of death is the fact that most people evidently have a

longing for more life. Even apart from questions of ultimate meaning and justice, they are simply not ready to have their personal stream of experience extinguished. Much modern thought has, to be sure, assumed this longing to be a sign of immaturity or simply a lingering after-effect of the traditional religions, which had allegedly created unrealistic expectations. The hope for continued life after death, in either case, has been treated as a problem that we will "get over."

This assumption, however, has not been borne out. Most people still believe in a life after death, or else they find their lack of belief a problem. Some philosophers who completely reject this belief candidly admit, in fact, that they wish that they could accept it. In any case, if this longing is a permanent feature of human existence as such, as it seems, then it raises a problem about the goodness of the universe: If there is no continued life beyond bodily death, as most modern thought assumes, then the universe has created an ineradicable desire in us that it will not fulfill—a conclusion that implies that the universe is not good. (By contrast, Whitehead often said in his Harvard classes, "The universe is fundamentally decent."[5])

Some years ago, a woman wrote a letter in *The New York Times* in which she expressed anger with the universe (I have been unable to find the letter). She was quite an accomplished person, but she had just learned that she was about to die. Assuming the truth of the modern view that death is the end, she was irate that she had spent so many years preparing for her profession and then all her knowledge and skill would simply disappear.

4. *Wholeness*: A fourth dimension of the problem created by our conscious anticipation of death involves the human religious desire for "salvation," in the sense of integrity or wholeness. Religious beliefs and practices are largely oriented around the sense that there is an ideal mode of existence, or a variety of ideal modes of existence, and that, through proper relation to the Holy Reality, we can realize, or have realized in us, such a mode of existence.

Most people, however, also have the sense of now being far from the goal, much too far for the gap to be traversed within the present life. The sense of this gap, between what we are and what we ought to be, has been closely connected to ideas of a life beyond the present one, in which this gap may be overcome. For strongly religious people, in other words, the desire for more life, discussed above, has been intimately related to a desire for a sanctified life.

If we believe that there is no life after death, however, then we seem forced to the conclusion that it is impossible for the ideal to be realized, at least for most people, because of insufficient time, which produces a dilemma: On the one hand, if we hold to the religious ideal, while assuming that it will never be realized, we in effect accept a form of Jean-Paul Sartre's view that the human being is a "useless passion," called to an ideal that cannot possibly be realized.[6]

On the other hand, in light of the widespread intuition that ought implies can, we may simply give up the religious ideal of wholeness, concluding that the old idea that human beings are called to realize such an ideal mode of existence was a colossal mistake. (Part of Immanuel Kant's reason for postulating life after death was that unless there would be time for us to develop the kind of virtuous character to which the moral law seems to call us, our confidence in the moral nature of the universe would be undermined.[7])

Objective Immortality

What does process philosophy say, or at least allow us to say, in the face of the distinctively human dimensions of the problem of death? A solution to the first dimension, that of ultimate meaning, is part and parcel of process philosophy's cosmology. With reference to what Whitehead called God's "consequent nature," Charles Hartshorne said:

> Deity is the highest possible form of the inclusion of others in the self.... Infallibly and with unrivaled adequacy aware of all others, God includes others—not, as we do, in a mostly indistinct or largely unconscious manner, but with full clarity.... Since God forgets nothing, loses no value once acquired, our entire worth is imperishable in the divine life.[8]

This doctrine of objective immortality is, most process thinkers would say, an essential part of an answer to the problems raised by our anticipation of death. But two questions remain. Is it, by itself, a sufficient answer?

And, if not, is it the only answer that process philosophy allows, or does it also allow for life after death?

With regard to this second question: The fact that Whitehead did not clearly affirm life after death, combined with the fact that Hartshorne explicitly denied it, has widely led to the conclusion that objective immortality is the only answer—beyond ordinary social immortality—allowed by process philosophy of religion to the problem created by our anticipation of death. Because of this assumption, process philosophy of religion and theology have been widely considered to provide an inadequate basis for theological reflection.

In addition, given the above analysis of the fourfold problem created by our anticipation of death, there is considerable justification for this response, because the doctrine of objective immortality answers, at most, only one aspect of this fourfold problem. It provides no answer to the problems created by the injustice of this life, the human desire for more life, and the desire for wholeness. These problems could be overcome, if at all, only in a life beyond bodily death.

It can also be argued, furthermore, that even the answer to the first problem, that of ultimate meaning, is unsatisfactory apart from belief in a continued existence beyond bodily death. Hartshorne argued that our awareness that we make a permanent contribution to the divine life should be sufficient. This argument, however, seems to reflect the bias of a privileged life, especially one in which there have been great opportunities to make contributions to other creatures, and thereby to God, with which one could be pleased. The subtitle of Hartshorne's autobiography, in fact, indicates that it involves reflections "upon his fortunate career."[9] For example, besides attending and then teaching in some of the finest educational institutions in the world, Hartshorne had a long and productive life, during which he published over 20 books and 500 essays. In a commentary on the scriptural idea that one's life should be a "reasonable, holy, and living sacrifice" to God, Hartshorne said "if I can inspire multitudes who will never see me in the flesh, then the incense I send up to God will continue to rise anew for many generations."[10]

Not everyone, however, can look back upon their lives, and the lives of their loved ones, with such satisfaction. Many individuals die young, before they have had an opportunity to make any significant contributions. Many other individuals have opportunities but waste them, either making no worthwhile contribution to others or, worse yet, being positively destructive of the lives of others, perhaps through theft, rape, murder, or selling drugs. These individuals often look back upon their lives with disgust. For such people, the message that our lives will be permanently retained in God will probably seem more like a threat than a promise: Better to be completely obliterated, such people may say, than to be a permanent blot on the divine memory! Although they may agree that the doctrine of the consequent nature of God provides life with a meaning, they may find it to be a horrible meaning.

Although the doctrine of objective immortality is necessary for a satisfactory solution to the distinctively human dimensions of the problem of death, it is not sufficient. It is necessary because, as Whitehead and Hartshorne held, the ultimate religious question is whether our lives are ultimately meaningful, and we can finally think of them as such only if we think of them as making a positive contribution to the Holy Reality. Apart from this assumption, life after death, even one that lasted forever, would ultimately be meaningless.

But the doctrine of objective immortality is not sufficient, because of the inadequacies discussed above.

These inadequacies could in principle be overcome, however, if the doctrine of objective immortality were combined with a doctrine of life after death. Such a doctrine would answer the simple desire that the present life be followed not by extinction, but by more life, in which new experiences are enjoyed, new adventures are had. It would also allow for the possibility that the injustices of the present life could be overcome, in the sense that all souls would have the opportunity to actualize their potentialities and to make amends for injustices to which they have contributed. It would also allow time for the religious ideal of ultimate wholeness to be realized. And, in allowing us to realize our various potentialities, a continuing life beyond bodily death would allow each of us to make a contribution to the Divine Reality of the universe with which we could be content, so that the doctrine of objective immortality would finally be the great source of joy that Hartshorne said it should be.

The next question, accordingly, is whether process philosophy allows for the possibility of life after death. It has widely been assumed that it does not, primarily for the two previously named reasons: the fact that Whitehead did not clearly affirm life after death and the fact that Hartshorne denied it.

Preview of Whitehead's Position

As will be discussed in Chapter 12, although Whitehead did not explicitly affirm life after death, he also did not deny it, saying instead that his philosophy is entirely neutral on the issue. Whitehead thereby meant that his doctrine of the human soul did not, like those of Plato and Descartes, entail that the soul would necessarily survive the death of the body, and also did not, like materialistic philosophies, rule out this possibility.

Whitehead also said that the question should be decided on "more special evidence, religious or otherwise." With this, he probably had in mind, besides reported events associated with religions, the evidence from psychical research. More on this later.

Hartshorne's Denial of Life after Death

In one of his last books, Hartshorne rejected "immortality as a career after death . . . in which our individual consciousnesses will have new experiences not enjoyed or suffered while on earth."[11] He even referred to that idea derisively, speaking of "tall tales about human careers after death."[12] As shown by these and many other passages, there is no doubt that Hartshorne explicitly rejected every form of belief that the human soul continues to have new experiences after bodily death.

Insofar as Hartshorne presented arguments for this rejection, however, they were arguments not against the idea of life after death as such, but only against the idea of *subjective immortality,* meaning that our conscious existence would literally continue forever. His rhetoric, accordingly, was usually directed against the idea that we would have "infinite careers" after death,[13] careers with "temporally infinite futures," careers that go on "forever."[14] His objections to this view are theological and metaphysical.

Hartshorne's theological argument is that belief in our subjective immortality tends "to make God a mere means for our everlasting happiness," "to make God the means to our ultimate fulfillment, as Kant did."[15]

Opposing this tendency was of extreme importance to Hartshorne, because for him the very meaning of life was to realize that it is our privilege to contribute to the life of God, "the only immortal being."[16] We will be unlikely to achieve this realization, Hartshorne believed, unless we accept our own temporal finitude.

Hartshorne's metaphysical argument against subjective immortality was based on the idea that "immortality is a divine trait."[17] The argument is that only the perfect being could have the "ability to preserve personal individuality through an infinity of experiences without monotony or loss of integrity."[18] In another formulation of this idea, Hartshorne said: "Each of us is a theme with variations. No theme other than that of the divine nature can admit an infinity of variations."[19] Because God is spatially ubiquitous while we "are mere fragments of the spatial whole," he also said it is unreasonable to think of ourselves as like God temporally, that is, as having "temporally infinite futures."[20]

Hartshorne's arguments did not say, accordingly, that the mind-body relation is such that life after death is impossible. He would have no philosophical argument, accordingly, against the idea that the human soul might exist for a very long time. Hartshorne did, in fact, concede in personal correspondence that his view of the mind-body relation makes survival possible.[21] Accordingly, as Hartshorne expert Donald Viney pointed out, his personal rejection of life after death did not mean that his philosophical position makes it impossible, as long as that extended life is not thought to be literally endless.[22]

It might be objected, to be sure, that such a view would not be satisfactory, that what we want assurance of is precisely that we will live forever. To make such a claim, however, would be to go far beyond our present knowledge. What we know, at most, is only that people, at least most people, want more life. We do not know that after having more life for a considerable period—perhaps ten thousand, a hundred thousand, a million, or a billion years—we would want to continue having new experiences. Perhaps there is truth in the Hindu and Buddhist notion of "karmic" existence, according to which we continue as finite centers of experience only insofar as we participate in this existence with intensity. That notion, in fact, is similar to Whitehead's view that enduring individuals continue to endure insofar as each member experiences that form of existence with intensity, passing it along to future members with appetition for its continuation. It might be, then, that we will continue to exist as long as we, at a deep level, want to continue. Besides allowing us the continued life that we want, life after death thus conceived would allow time for souls to actualize all their potentialities, to reach a state of wholeness, and thereby to have their lives finally make a contribution to the divine life with which they can be content.

There is nothing in process philosophy, accordingly, to prevent the affirmation of a kind of life after death in which the distinctively human problems of death would find their resolution. Such an affirmation would strengthen process philosophy's theodicy, a task to which I have devoted considerable attention.[23]

Endnotes

1. Alfred North Whitehead, *Process and Reality: An Essay in Cosmology*, Corrected Edition, ed. David Ray Griffin and Donald W. Sherburne (New York: Free Press), 340.
2. Charles Hartshorne, *The Logic of Perfection* (LaSalle, IL: Open Court, 1962), 132.
3. *Religion in the Making*, Introduction by Judith A. Jones (New York: Fordham University Press, 1996), 41; this edition repeated the pagination of the original edition of the book, published by Macmillan in 1926.
4. Immanuel Kant, *Critique of Practical Reason*. See also "Immanuel Kant: The Immortality of the Soul," from *Outline of Great Books*, Vol. 1, ed. J. A. Hammerton (New York: William H. Wise, 1934).
5. Victor Lowe, *Alfred North Whitehead: The Man and His Work*, Vol. II (Baltimore and London: Johns Hopkins Press, 1990), 244.
6. John Paul Sartre, *Being and Nothingness* (New York: Philosophical Library, 1956); originally *L'être et le néant* (1943).
7. Kant, *Critique of Practical Reason*; "Immanuel Kant: The Immortality of the Soul."
8. Charles Hartshorne, *Omnipotence and Other Theological Mistakes* (Albany, NY: SUNY Press, 1984), 110.

9. Charles Hartshorne, *The Darkness and the Light: A Philosopher Reflects Upon His Fortunate Career and Those Who Made It Possible* (Albany, NY: SUNY Press, 1990).
10. Hartshorne, *The Logic of Perfection*, 257–58.
11. Hartshorne, *Omnipotence and Other Theological Mistakes*, 4.
12. Hartshorne, *Omnipotence and Other Theological Mistakes*, 117.
13. Hartshorne, *Omnipotence and Other Theological Mistakes*, 47, 48, 117.
14. Hartshorne, *Omnipotence and Other Theological Mistakes*, 36, 40.
15. Hartshorne, *Omnipotence and Other Theological Mistakes*, 117; Charles Hartshorne, *Creative Synthesis and Philosophic Method* (University Press of America, 1970), 289.
16. Hartshorne, *Omnipotence and Other Theological Mistakes*, 117.
17. Hartshorne, *Creative Synthesis and Philosophic Method*, 289.
18. Hartshorne, *The Logic of Perfection*, 261.
19. Hartshorne, *The Logic of Perfection*, 261.
20. Hartshorne, *Omnipotence and Other Theological Mistakes*, 36.
21. Letter from Hartshorne to David Griffin in 1994.
22. Donald Wayne Viney, *Charles Hartshorne and the Existence of God* (Albany, NY: SUNY Press, 1985), 116.
23. David Ray Griffin, *God, Power, and Evil: A Process Theodicy* (Philadelphia: Westminster, 1976); reprinted with a new preface (Louisville: Westminster John Knox, 2004; *Evil Revisited: Responses and Reconsiderations* (Albany, NY: SUNY Press, 1991); "Traditional Free Will Theodicy and Process Theodicy: Hasker's Claim for Parity," *Process Studies* 29/2 (Fall-Winter 2000), 209–26; "Creation out of Nothing, Creation Out of Chaos, and the Problem of Evil," in *Encountering Evil: Live Options in Theodicy*, 2nd edition, ed. Stephen T. Davis (Louisville: Westminster John Knox, 2001), 108–25; "Process Theodicy and Climate Change," in *The History of Evil: From the Mid-20th Century to Today,* Jerome Gellman et al., (Durham, UK: Acumen Publishing, 2018).

CHAPTER TWO

The Case against Life after Death

THE TRADITIONAL BASIS for hope was belief in life after death. Modern culture, however, has so diminished this belief that today, in educated circles, it is largely assumed that life after death is an outmoded belief. Accordingly, modern people have had to find another source for hope. For traditional Christians, Jews, and Muslims, of course, God—understood as loving and omnipotent—could be expected to give us renewed life after death. However, for liberal members of these religions, this way of thinking has lost credibility. There are simply far too many reasons to reject the traditional idea of divine omnipotence.[1] And besides this loss of belief in divine omnipotence, many liberal members of these religions have been infected by the widespread materialism of modern culture. An example of materialism's implications for the question of life after death is provided in a book entitled *The Illusion of Immortality* by philosopher Corliss Lamont,[2] who taught at Columbia University.

Belief in life after death was an illusion, Lamont said, because "the probabilities against a future life for the individual are so overwhelming."[3] Indeed, he spoke even more strongly, calling life beyond bodily death "an impossibility."[4]

The basic reason for Lamont's conclusion involved the mind-body relation: "The fundamental issue lies," said Lamont, "in the relationship between body and soul." Modern science, he claimed, has shown that the mind is simply a function of the brain.[5]

Materialism rules out life after death, Lamont pointed out, because it would require a resurrected body, and this claim would presuppose the idea of a supernatural intervention by an omnipotent deity, which is ruled out by a science-based cosmology.[6]

According to the modern worldview, there are only two possible positions on the mind-body relation, materialism and dualism. Because mind-body dualism is false, Lamont concluded that materialism must be true. But whereas Lamont correctly said that dualism is a nonstarter (I support this opinion in Appendix II), he failed to acknowledge that materialism, which he endorsed, is at least equally problematic. The basic problem is how a brain, composed entirely of insentient particles, could produce consciousness.

Although Lamont was right to say that dualism cannot be used to show the possibility of life after death, materialism is too inadequate and incoherent to provide a basis for arguing that life after death is impossible.

Endnotes

1. David Ray Griffin, *God Exists but Gawd Does Not: From Evil to New Atheism to Fine-Tuning* (Anoka, MN: Process Century Press, 2016), Part 1.
2. Corliss Lamont, *The Illusion of Immortality*, 4th ed. (New York: Frederick Ungar, 1965). The case against life after death has more recently been made in *The Myth of an Afterlife: The Case against Life After Death*, ed. by Michael Martin and Keith Augustine (Lanham, MD: Rowman & Littlefield Publishers, 2015). But I find the older book to be more helpful in stating the basic case.
3. Lamont, *The Illusion of Immortality*, vii.
4. Lamont, *The Illusion of Immortality*, viii.
5. Lamont, *The Illusion of Immortality*, 24.
6. Lamont, *The Illusion of Immortality*, 7, 51.

CHAPTER THREE

Bacteria and the Mind-Body Problem

A NEW, POSTMODERN worldview is necessary to deal adequately with many, many issues.[1] Central to these is the mind-body relation. This chapter and the next show how it can be solved by the doctrine of pan-experientialism, also called panpsychism.

The Mind-Body Relation

As shown in Chapter 4 and Appendix II, conventional treatments of the relation of the mind to its body, including its brain, are completely inadequate. Surprisingly, recent microbiology has shown how the presumed alternatives of dualism and materialism can be transcended.

The brain is constituted of brain cells, called neurons. According to the conventional views, the neurons are mere matter in Descartes's sense—that is, devoid of experience or sentience. This view was expressed in a rhetorical question by one-time Oxford philosopher Colin McGinn:

> How could the aggregation of millions of individually insentient neurons generate subjective awareness?[2]

McGinn's book *The Problem of Consciousness* centers around the fact that this is an unanswerable question.

But what if the neurons are not insentient? What if they have their own experiences, only at a much lower level than ours? What if scientists had recently discovered the Descartes-McGinn view of the brain to be false?

Decision-Making Bacteria

That is exactly what has happened. In the 1970s, a few scientists started reporting that bacteria, the lowest form of life, make decisions on the basis of receiving information from their environments. For example, a 1974 article in the journal *Science* was entitled "Decision-Making in Bacteria."[3]

By now, this then-startling idea has become commonplace, with many journal articles reporting experiments verifying the idea. For example, articles with the following titles appeared in more recent years:

> "Bacteria Provide New Insights into Human Decision Making" (2009).
>
> "Bacteria Use Chat to Play the 'Prisoner's Dilemma' Game in Deciding Their Fate" (2012).
>
> "How Do Bacteria Make Decisions?" (2014).[4]

The last of these three articles began:

> Decision making is not limited to animals like humans or birds. Bacteria also make decisions with intricate precision.... Bacteria have a memory albeit short.[5]

The discovery that experience, memory, and decision-making occur in cells is a major development in recent microbiology. According to University of Chicago microbiologist James Shapiro, "Cells are capable of sophisticated information processing."[6] Even the smallest cells, he said, "use sophisticated sensory and intracellular communication processes to discriminate between alternative nutrients."[7]

Sentient Cells vs. Mind-Body Mystery

Famous and once-controversial biologist Lynn Margulis (who died prematurely in 2011) is best known for her theory of "symbiogenesis," which began with her discovery that the eukaryotic cell is a composite resulting from a symbiotic union of primitive prokaryotic cells. In other words, eukaryotes emerged when large prokaryotes absorbed smaller ones.

Widely recognized as the most gifted evolutionary biologist of her generation, Margulis was a Distinguished University Professor at the University of Massachusetts, Amherst. She was elected to the National Academy of Sciences in 1983 and to the Russian Academy of Natural Sciences in 1997. She was awarded the National Medal of Science in 1999 and received the Darwin-Wallace Medal in 2008.

Although her worldview differed radically from that of British evolutionary biologist Richard Dawkins, who had long ridiculed her views, he eventually called her discovery "one of the great achievements of twentieth-century evolutionary biology." Likewise, Niles Eldredge, an American biologist, wrote: "Lynn was put down as having had a really crazy idea.... Now it's taught in all the textbooks as the self-evident truth."[8]

Her theory of symbiogenesis was based on the idea that all living organisms are sentient. Saying that her worldview "recognizes the perceptive capacity of all live beings,"[9] she held that "consciousness is a property of all living cells," even the most elementary ones: "Bacteria are conscious. These bacterial beings have been around since the origin of life."[10]

Although some of us may prefer to save the term "consciousness" for higher types of experience, the crucial point is that all cells have perceptive experience, rather than being, as McGinn (like Descartes) believed, "insensate matter." Alluding to how this new view can dissolve the traditional mind-body problem, Margulis said:

> Thought and behavior in people are rendered far less mysterious when we realize that choice and sensitivity are already exquisitely developed in the microbial cells that became our ancestors.[11]

The assumption of materialists and dualists alike was that neurons are insentient. But neurons, being eukaryotes, are far more complex and sophisticated than prokaryotes, such as bacteria. So, dualists and materialists are behind the times scientifically, assuming neurons to be insentient, even though microbiology has shown since the 1970s that bacteria, which are much more primitive than neurons, are fully sentient. Microbiology has dissolved the mind-body problem.

Similarly, Margulis said that the joining together of individuals at one level can create "a new whole that was, in effect, far greater than the sum of its parts."[12] The basic issue, she said, is how "independent, separate organisms fuse to form new individuals."[13] Margulis's language was similar to that of Charles Hartshorne. Whereas he spoke of "compound individuals," to be discussed below, she used the term "composite individuality" to describe the "transition from bacterial to eukaryotic genomes."[14]

This revolutionary view of bacteria is a central element in the new worldview that is needed. The need for such a worldview has been expressed by one of our leading philosophers, Thomas Nagel, emeritus professor of New York University. In his great 2012 book *Mind and Cosmos*, he wrote that to understand how we "descended from bacteria," we must think of natural entities as "something more than physical all the way down." In other words, a fully naturalistic worldview requires some version of panpsychism, according to which "organisms with mental life are not miraculous anomalies but an integral part of nature."[15]

To make a more general point: A universe in which bacteria can naturally turn into creatures such as us is—pretty amazing.

Endnotes

1. For the sense in which the new worldview is "postmodern," see Appendix I.

2. Colin McGinn, *The Problem of Consciousness: Essays Toward a Resolution* (Oxford: Basil Blackwell, 1991), 1.

3. Julius Adler and Wung-Wai Tso, "Decision-Making in Bacteria," *Science* 184 (1974): 1292-94.

4. Kim McDonald, "Bacteria Provide New Insights into Human Decision Making," UC San Diego, 8 December 2009; "Bacteria Use Chat to Play the 'Prisoner's Dilemma' Game in Deciding Their Fate," *American Chemical Society*, 27 May 2012); Matthew Russell, "How Do

Bacteria Make Decisions?" *Frontiers*, 23 January 2014.

5. Russell, "How Do Bacteria Make Decisions?" Additional articles include M. Gomelski and W. D. Hoff, "Light Helps Bacteria Make Important Lifestyle Decisions," *Trends in Microbiology*," 19 September 2011, and Daniel M. Cornforth, et al., "Combinatorial Quorum Sensing Allows Bacteria to Resolve Their Social and Physical Environment," *Proceedings of the National Academy of Sciences*, 4 March 2014.

6. James A. Shapiro, "Transposable Elements as the Key to a 21st Century View of Evolution," *Genetica*, 107: 171–70 (1999).

7. James Shapiro, "Cell Cognition and Cell Decision-Making," Huffington Post, 19 March 2012.

8. Richard Dawkins, "A Survival Machine," and Niles Eldridge, "A Battle of Words," both in John Brockman, *The Third Culture: Beyond the Scientific Revolution* (New York: Simon & Schuster, 1995).

9. Lynn Margulis, "Gaia and Machines," in *Back to Darwin: A Richer Account of Evolution,* ed. John B. Cobb, Jr. (Grand Rapids, MI: Eerdmans, 2007), 167-75, at 172.

10. Dick Teresi, "Lynn Margulis Says She's Not Controversial, She's Right," *Discover Magazine*, April 2011.

11. Lynn Margulis, "Gaia Is a Tough Bitch," Chap. 7 of Brockman, *The Third Culture.*

12. Margulis, "Gaia Is a Tough Bitch."

13. Lynn Margulis and Dorion Sagan, *Acquiring Genomes: A Theory of the Origins of Species* (New York: Basic Books, 2003), 97.

14. Lynn Margulis, "Serial Endosymbiotic Theory (SET) and Composite Individuality: Transition from Bacterial to Eukaryotic Genomes," *Microbiology Today* 31 (2004): 172–74.

15. Thomas Nagel, *Mind and Cosmos: Why the Materialist Neo-Darwinian Conception of Nature Is Almost Certainly False* (Oxford University Press, 2012), 30, 34, 53, 57.

CHAPTER FOUR

Panpsychism or Panexperientialism

The discovery that bacteria and other prokaryotes have experience, we have seen, provides a scientific basis for overcoming the traditional mind-body problem. But how are we to understand the emergence in the evolutionary process of prokaryotic cells, with their experience, themselves? If it is held that they emerge out of insentient components, we would have a new "mind-body problem," only at a lower level. However, there is good reason to hold that the prokaryotic cell, with its level of experience, emerged from incorporating entities with still lower levels of sentience.

A team of microbiologists have spoken of "decision-making at a subcellular level."[1] The most complex components of prokaryotic cells are their organelles, so the authors' reference to "subcellular decision-making" would evidently refer to decisions made by organelles. We could then assume that organelles themselves emerged out of entities with still lower-level experiences, and so on down.

A view similar to that of Margulis had earlier been worked out by philosophers William James, Alfred North Whitehead, and Charles Hartshorne. Whitehead called his position "the philosophy of organism," in which he spoke of complex organisms as "organisms of organisms."

Electrons and hydrogen nuclei are, he said, quite elementary organisms; then "the atoms, and the molecules, are organisms of a higher type, which also represent a compact definite organic unity." Still more complex are "individual living beings."[2]

Whitehead was likely influenced on this issue by William James, who probably lay behind Whitehead's position on "concrete entities." Speaking of "a concrete bit of personal experience," James said: "It is a full fact," being "of the kind to which all realities whatsoever must belong." Our feeling, said James, "is the one thing that fills up the measure of our concrete actuality." He continued: "[Hermann] Lotze's doctrine that the only meaning we can attach to the notion of a thing as it is 'in itself' is by conceiving it as it is for itself; i.e., as a piece of full experience."[3] Moreover, James explicitly said that "pluralistic panpsychism" was his worldview.[4]

As stated in the previous chapter, a term for Lynn Margulis's idea that "independent, separate organisms fuse to form new individuals" was provided many years earlier by Hartshorne in a 1936 essay entitled "The Compound Individual."[5] The basic idea was that one individual, such as an atom, can be present in a more complex individual, such as a molecule, which can in turn be present in a still more complex individual, such as a macromolecule, which can in turn be present in the still more complex individual that we call an organelle, which in turn is present in the prokaryotic call, such as a bacterium. Prokaryotic cells can then be compounded to form the more complex eukaryotic cells, which can then form still more complex individuals, such as flies, squirrels, and humans.

Although Margulis as a biologist limited her discussion to living cells, the idea that the components of the cells must themselves have sentience would be consonant with her outlook, so that nature would contain compound individuals, in the Whiteheadian-Hartshornean sense, all the way down to the simplest entities discussed by physicists. (I had become friends with Margulis. One of my great regrets is that I did not get a chance to talk to her about this issue before she suddenly died.)

This view, that experience goes all the way down, is best called "panexperientialism." Although this position, under the older name "panpsychism," was long derided, it is now gaining adherents. According to the Wikipedia article on Panpsychism, "The recent interest in the hard problem of consciousness has once again made panpsychism a mainstream theory."[6]

This new interest was exemplified by the publication of a major book in 2016 entitled *Panpsychism: Contemporary Perspectives*.[7] Here are two recent philosophers who have affirmed this position.

Thomas Nagel

Panpsychism or panexperientialism has long been advocated by the previously introduced Thomas Nagel, who argued that the mind-body relation is impossible to understand on the assumption that the brain is composed of purely physical entities, devoid of experience.[8] Agreeing with neo-Darwinism that a theory of evolution must be naturalistic, he said that we need "a naturalistic expansion of evolutionary theory to account for consciousness."[9] This expansion involves rejecting "psychophysical reductionism," according to which the mind can be reduced to the brain understood in a Cartesian sense. Repeating what was said at the end of the previous chapter, because we need a way to understand how we "descended from bacteria," we must think of natural entities as "something more than physical all the way down." In other words, a fully naturalistic worldview requires some version of panpsychism, according to which "organisms with mental life are not miraculous anomalies but an integral part of nature."[10]

Besides affirming panpsychism in general, Nagel approvingly cited both Whitehead and Hartshorne. With regard to Whitehead, Nagel endorsed his idea that philosophers should not equate the "abstractions of physics with the whole of reality," but should regard "concrete entities, all the way down to the level of electrons," as "embodying a standpoint on the world"—that is, as having experience. With regard to Hartshorne, Nagel described an essay by him on "the place of mind in nature," in which Hartshorne affirmed panpsychism, as an "acute and historically informed discussion."[11]

Galen Strawson

Another major philosopher who has adopted a panexperientialist position is Galen Strawson (the son of the famous British philosopher Peter F. Strawson), who now teaches at the University of Texas, Austin.

Saying that the intractability of the mind-body problem has been due to the inadequacy of traditional philosophers' concept of the physical (not the mental), Strawson said: "The descriptive scheme of physics...will have to change dramatically," giving us "a qualitative-character-of-experience physics."[12]

In a 2015 essay arguing for "the primacy of panpsychism," Strawson discussed "compelling reasons for favoring panpsychism above all other positive substantive proposals about the fundamental nature of concrete reality." Strawson added that he uses the terms "panpsychism" and "panexperientialism" interchangeably.[13]

Whiteheadian panexperientialism is discussed much more fully in Appendix II.

Endnotes

1. Lanying Zeng et al., "Decision Making at a Subcellular Level Determines the Outcome of Bacteriophage Infection," *Cell* 141: 682–91 (14 May 2010).
2. Whitehead, *Science and the Modern World* (New York: Free Press, [1925] 1967), 110.
3. William James, *The Varieties of Religious Experience* (London: Colliers, 1961), 387.
4. Ralph Barton Perry, *The Thought and Character of William James* (New York: Colliers, 1961), 387.
5. Charles Hartshorne, "The Compound Individual," in *Philosophical Essays for Alfred North Whitehead,* ed. Otis Lee (New York: Longmans, Green & Co., 1936). Reprinted in Hartshorne, *Whitehead's Philosophy: Selected Essays, 1936–1970* (University of Nebraska Press, 1972).
6. "Panpsychism," Wikipedia, accessed January 2015. Philosophers who had made panpsychism a somewhat mainstream theory in earlier times included Wilhelm Gottfried Leibniz, Henri Bergson, Herman Lotze, William James, and Charles Peirce, while scientists included Charles Birch, David Bohm, Bernard Rensch, C. H. Waddington, and Sewall Wright (all of these scientists had essays in *Mind in Nature: Essays on the Interface of Science and Philosophy,* ed. John B. Cobb, Jr., and David Ray Griffin (Washington, DC: University Press of America, 1977).

7. Godehard Brüntrup and Ludwig Jaskolla, *Panpsychism: Contemporary Perspectives* (Oxford University Press, 2016).
8. Thomas Nagel, "What Is It Like to be a Bat?" *Mortal Questions* (Cambridge University Press, 1979).
9. Nagel, *Mind and Cosmos: Why the Materialist Neo-Darwinian Conception of Nature Is Almost Certainly False* (Oxford University Press, 2012), 48.
10. Nagel, *Mind and Cosmos*, 30, 34, 53, 57.
11. Nagel, *Mind and Cosmos*, 33, referring to Charles Hartshorne, "Physics and Psychics: The Place of Mind in Nature," in *Mind in Nature,* ed. Cobb and Griffin, 89–96.
12. Galen Strawson, *Mental Reality* (MIT Press, 1994), 89, 99, 104. See also a book devoted to Strawson's developing position: Galen Strawson et al., *Consciousness and Its Place in Nature: Does Physicalism Entail Panpsychism?*, ed. Anthony Freeman (Exeter, UK: Imprint Academic, [2006] 2010).
13. Galen Strawson, "Mind and Being: The Primacy of Panpsychism," in *Panpsychism: Contemporary Perspectives*, ed. G. Brünstup and L. Jaskolla (Oxford University Press, 2015).

CHAPTER FIVE

James, Whitehead, and Psychical Research

THE SOCIETY FOR PSYCHICAL RESEARCH (SPR) was founded in 1882 in London. According to its charter, it was founded

> to investigate that large body of debatable phenomena designated by such terms as mesmeric, psychical and spiritualistic ... in the same spirit of exact and unimpassioned enquiry which has enabled Science to solve so many problems.[1]

In its early days, the membership rolls read like a Who's Who of British intelligentsia, such as then-British prime minister William Gladstone, who said that psychical research was "the most important work, which is being done in the world..., by far the most important."[2] Other major figures included Gerald and Arthur Balfour (minister of Parliament and prime minister, respectively), Leslie Stephen, Alfred Tennyson, John Ruskin, and Nobel Prize-winning physiologist Charles Richet.[3]

Such people signed up primarily because Cambridge moral philosopher Henry Sidgwick (1838–1900), who was generally considered the most honest man in England, was the president. Indeed, some of the members had joined the SPR only on the condition that Sidgwick would be the president. British philosopher C. D. Broad wrote:

> The fact that Sidgwick, whose reputation for sanity, truthfulness, and fairness was well known to everyone who mattered in England, was at the head of the Society gave it an intellectual and moral status which was invaluable at the time.[4]

Although several intellectuals supported psychical research, the majority did not. (For example, American psychologist Edward Titchener of Cornell University declared: "No scientifically-minded psychologist believes in telepathy.") Like William James, Henry Sidgwick's SPR wanted to establish sufficient evidence to allow psychical research to be recognized as a new science. With this goal in mind, James paraphrased a statement by Sidgwick in which he had expressed frustrations at the current state of affairs:

> The divided state of public opinion on all these matters was a scandal to science, absolute disdain on a priori grounds characterizing what may be called professional opinion, whilst completely uncritical and indiscriminate credulity was too often amongst those who pretended to have a first-hand acquaintance with the facts.[5]

The context for this founding was the fact that religion was under siege from nineteenth-century science, which tended to portray the world as purposeless and meaningless. Sidgwick wanted to use better science to portray a "friendly universe."[6]

The types of phenomena studied by psychical research are usually divided into three types: (1) extrasensory perception (such as telepathy), meaning the reception of information by a mind without the use of any of the physical senses; (2) psychokinesis, meaning influence exerted by a mind without employing its body; and (3) evidence for life after death, meaning the continuation of a mind or soul after the death of its physical body. The present chapter focuses on extrasensory perception, with an eye toward its relevance for the possibility of life after death.

Extrasensory Perception

The reality of extrasensory perception is controversial, but not because of the absence of good evidence for it. Rather, it is controversial because it is in strong tension with the modern worldview, of which there have been two versions.

The Modern Worldview: First Version

The first version of the modern worldview was created in the seventeenth century by thinkers such as Marin Mersenne, René Descartes, Robert Boyle, and Isaac Newton. This worldview had a mechanistic doctrine of nature, a dualistic view of the human being (with a material body and a nonphysical soul), and a supernatural deity.

A supernatural deity was deemed necessary to explain how the physical body, held to be composed of insentient matter, and the nonphysical soul, composed of consciousness, could interact. In other words, given the idea that body and soul are different in kind, it was impossible to understand how they could interact: How could a spiritual mind or soul influence the body, and how could the mechanistic body in turn influence the mind or soul?

Central to modernity has been the question of "action at a distance," of which there has been a long discussion.[7] In the first version of the modern worldview in the seventeenth and eighteenth centuries, the mechanical philosophers agreed "that the program of natural philosophy lay in demonstrating that the phenomena of nature are produced by the mutual interplay of material particles which act on each other by direct contact alone."[8] For example, "the fundamental tenet of Descartes' mechanical philosophy of nature [was] that one body can act on another only by direct contact."[9] Events involving apparent action at a distance do occur, but only through the supernatural power of God.

This modern, mechanical worldview was articulated in opposition to a wild assortment of Neoplatonic, Hermetic, Cabalistic, and naturalistic philosophies that had spread northward from the Platonic Renaissance that began in Italy in the fifteenth century. Some of these were "magical" philosophies, which allowed action at a distance. They specifically allowed the human mind to exert and receive influence at a distance—for example, through "sympathy." These philosophies implied, and some of their proponents explicitly argued, that the miracles of the New Testament (and, for Catholics, the ongoing Christian tradition) were purely natural effects, not different in kind from extraordinary events that have occurred in other traditions and not requiring any supernatural intervention. Defenders of

Christianity saw these philosophies as posing a profound threat, because the appeal to miracles as the sign of God's establishment of Christianity as the one true religion was the central element in Christian apologetics.[10]

Father Marin Mersenne, who was—along with Descartes—the central figure in the establishment of the modern, mechanistic philosophy in scientific, philosophical, and theological circles in France, advocated the mechanistic philosophy on these grounds. Because it showed that no influence at a distance could occur naturally, the miracles that occurred in the New Testament and later Christian history were really miracles—that is, they required the supernatural intervention of God.[11]

As discussed in Chapter 4, the mechanistic view of nature made the mind-body relation mysterious. This mystery was reinforced by the other main doctrine of the modern worldview: the sensationist doctrine of perception, according to which we can perceive things beyond our own minds only by means of our physical senses. Accordingly, there can be no telepathy or evidence for life after death—or, for that matter, no experiential basis for ethical, aesthetic, or religious experience.

Descartes answered the question of how body and soul are related by appealing to divine omnipotence.[12] "For thinkers of that age," observed William James, "'God' was the great solvent of all absurdities."[13] There are still supernaturalists who give this explanation. According to former Oxford philosopher Richard Swinburne:

> Science cannot explain the evolution of a mental life.... God, an omnipotent, omniscient, perfectly free and perfectly good source of all ... [could] explain the otherwise mysterious mind-body connection.... God, being omnipotent, would have the power to produce a soul thus interacting.[14]

The first version of the modern worldview is still the view of conservative Christian churches, who continue to use the so-called mental miracles of Jesus to prove the unique truth and saving power of Christian faith. Accordingly, psychical research, with its position that extrasensory perception is a fully natural capacity, is threatening to this type of Christianity.

The Modern Worldview: Second Version

The scientific community did not long remain with the first version of the modern worldview. Coming to find it distasteful to need to refer to a supernatural agent to explain natural phenomena, and coming to consider ridiculous the idea that such an agent could interrupt natural laws, the scientific community created a new version of the modern worldview. In this new version, the mechanistic view of nature was retained. But mind-body dualism was replaced by "epiphenomenalism," according to which the mind is called "real" although it cannot affect the body, even the brain.[15]

This view was in turn replaced by complete materialism, according to which the mind and the brain are in some sense identical (the position is known as "identism"), so there is no mind or soul distinct from the brain. This mechanistic, materialistic worldview has been accepted as the "modern scientific worldview" since the late nineteenth century.

This new scientific worldview required the epistemology known as "sensate empiricism." Empiricism as such is the sensible doctrine that no entities should be affirmed except those that can be experienced—an epistemology that should obviously be the basis for making scientific statements. But the adjective "sensate" adds the insistence on "sensationism"—the doctrine that we can have no experience of anything beyond our own minds except by means of our physical senses. Although John Locke and David Hume are often simply called "empiricists," what they initiated was *sensate* empiricism.

Responding to scientific and philosophical questions by appealing to supernaturalism is no longer acceptable in science and science-based philosophy, which in the nineteenth and twentieth centuries concluded that there can be no interruptions of the normal cause-effect relations. In fact, naturalism, in the basic sense of the rejection of supernaturalism, is now the fundamental philosophical presupposition of science. Accordingly, any discussion of mind-body interactions must be carried out within a naturalistic worldview, meaning one in which there are no miracles requiring divine intervention.

Psychical research is naturalistic in this sense. It portrays extrasensory perception as a wholly natural, if in some respects extraordinary, phenomenon. But scientists and philosophers who have internalized the second version of the modern worldview have regarded extrasensory perception as anti-scientific, impossible, absurd, superstitious. Although these philosophers and scientists tend to treat psychical research as if it implied supernaturalism, they evidently have failed to realize that the opposite is the truth: It gives naturalistic answers to questions that modernist philosophers could answer only by appeals to supernaturalism. For example, if Jesus had the ability to know the thoughts of other people, this fact would provide no evidence for his divinity, or even for the idea that a supernatural deity was working through him.

Sensationism ruled out in advance the position of the psychical research community, according to which the form of non-sensory perception called "extrasensory perception" is fully natural. From the perspective of sensationism, the ability of Jesus to "read minds" had to be considered either supernatural, as conservative theists generally hold, or simply impossible, as the scientific and science-based philosophical communities have generally held. In either case, psychical research is dismissed as a pseudoscience.

The Pseudoscience Charge

According to both James and Whitehead, affirming empiricism requires taking account of every kind of experience. This means at least that a philosophical worldview, to be adequate, must deal with all the sciences. This means that it must take account of the evidence that James called "the phenomena of psychic research so-called." But late modern science has generally denied this, by declaring that psychical research is not a true science, but merely a pseudoscience.

To deal with this issue, it is necessary to introduce the term parapsychology. This term refers to the types of psychical research that are carried out in laboratories or other settings that can be tightly controlled. What response could be made to the charge that parapsychology is simply a pseudoscience, so that real scientists can ignore it?

One possible response involves the attempt to formulate criteria for establishing a "line of demarcation" between science and pseudoscience—a line that would show all generally recognized sciences to be in the former category and all the disliked fields, such as parapsychology, to be in the latter. However, scholars in sociology and the philosophy of science have concluded that this attempt proved to be a failure.[16]

One reason for this failure is that the argument is often circular. For example, psychologist Ray Hyman of the University of Oregon, who had his own reasons for rejecting parapsychological beliefs, criticized the criteria used by Canadian psychologist James Alcock, writing: "The categories of both science and pseudoscience are fuzzy.... It looks very much like the criteria themselves were chosen in order to exclude parapsychology."[17]

Nevertheless, the conviction that parapsychology cannot possibly be considered one of the sciences remains, mainly because of the conviction that parapsychology's alleged phenomena conflict with science.

In a book entitled *Parapsychology: Science or Magic?* James Alcock said: "Parapsychology is indistinguishable from pseudo-science, because genuine parapsychological occurrences would imply a 'relationship between consciousness and the physical world radically different from that held to be possible by contemporary science.'"[18]

Physicist John Wheeler, upset that the Parapsychological Association was accepted as a member of the American Association for the Advancement of Science, called on the members of the AAAS to "drive the pseudos out of the workshop of science."[19]

Philosopher Antony Flew, also calling parapsychology a pseudoscience, argued that the Parapsychological Association should be "politely disaffiliated" from the American Association for the Advancement of Science.[20]

In an essay asking "Is Parapsychology a Science?" philosopher Paul Kurtz said that its findings "contradict the general conceptual framework of scientific knowledge."[21]

In an essay entitled "Science and the Supernatural," George Price relegated the phenomena of parapsychology to the category of the "supernatural"—by which he meant the nonexistent—on the grounds that "parapsychology and modern science are incompatible."[22]

Science As Mechanistic

According to this argument, parapsychology cannot possibly be a science, because it conflicts with some of the fundamental principles of modern science. In what way does it allegedly conflict with science? The main ground for this claim is that science is necessarily mechanistic.

Making his well-known claim—"The essence of science is mechanism. The essence of magic is animism"—George Price argued that a scientific claim about some phenomenon requires the possibility of "a detailed mechanistic explanation."[23]

Anthony Flew stated that the decisive objection to parapsychology's alleged phenomena is the lack of a "conceivable mechanism."[24]

Psychologist Donald Hebb, saying that parapsychologists have "offered enough evidence to have convinced us on almost any other issue," admitted that his reason for rejecting it "is—in a literal sense—prejudice," adding that he could have found the evidence convincing if he had "some guess as to the mechanics of the disputed process."[25]

In insisting that science as such is mechanistic, these scientists have misunderstood the nature of science. "Science means, first of all," said William James, "a certain dispassionate method." It is not "a certain set of results that one should pin one's faith upon and hug forever."[26]

Basic Limiting Principles

The mechanistic frame of mind has also been illustrated in a response of philosopher Jane Duran to C. D. Broad, a highly respected British philosopher. Broad had developed a list of "basic limiting principles," meaning ones that have been widely accepted as limiting what is credible. One of these principles, Broad pointed out, is this one:

> Any event that is said to cause another event (the second event being referred to as an 'effect') must be related to the effect through some causal chain.[27]

Having studied psychical research, Broad argued that the evidence for telepathy was strong enough to reject this principle. Duran, however, said:

> The absence of a specifiable and recognizably causal chain seems to constitute a difficult, if not insurmountable, objection to our giving a coherent account of what it means to make such a claim. As long, at least, as our ordinary notions of causality remain intact, there seem to be strong philosophical reasons for concluding that telepathy [is] not possible.[28]

Duran's argument simply begged the question. The dispute between her and Broad could be summarized thus:

- *Limiting Principle*: All causation between noncontiguous events is transmitted by a chain of contiguous events.

- *Broad's Response*: Parapsychology shows that sometimes an event is affected by a noncontiguous event directly, without being mediated by a chain of contiguous events.
- *Duran's Counter-response*: We know that Broad's claim is false, because all causation between noncontiguous events is transmitted by a chain of contiguous events.

As illustrated by the statements of Price, Flew, Hebb, and Duran, the main reason to consider psi (a term for parapsychological events) impossible is the belief that science is necessarily and completely mechanistic. This dogma entails that there could be no influence at a distance—such as telepathy, which means "feeling at a distance."

William James was one scientist who did not agree with this "scientific critique" of psychical research. James rejected sensate empiricism in favor of "a thicker and more radical empiricism," which included, in his words, "the phenomena of psychic research so-called."[29]

James's Radical Empiricism and Psychical Research

We need a scientific worldview, James argued, that would allow these phenomena to be regarded as fully natural, albeit exceptional, occurrences. He wrote:

> Science, so far as science denies such exceptional occurrences, lies prostrate in the dust for me; and the most urgent intellectual need which I feel at present is that science be built up again in a form in which such things may have a positive place.[30]

James's first intellectual biographer, Ralph Barton Perry, wrote in 1935:

> James's interest in "psychical research" was not one of his vagaries, but was central and typical.[31]

Some recent biographers of James have written as if he did not deal with psychical research, or at least that it was not important to him. They were evidently embarrassed by the fact that their hero dealt seriously with a topic they considered disreputable. However, this was emphatically not the case with Robert D. Richardson's 2006 intellectual biography, *William James: In the Maelstrom of American Modernism*.[32]

This view has also been endorsed by a 2007 book by Krister Dylan Knapp, *William James: Psychical Research and the Challenge of Modernity*. Knapp said:

> Psychical research permeated William James's life and thought, for nearly thirty years, from the early 1880s until his death in 1910. James immersed himself in the field.... His professional commitment to psychical research began during a winter trip to England in 1882, when members of the Society for Psychical Research (SPR) befriended him, and in 1884–85, when he expedited the founding of the SPR's sister organization in Boston, the American Society for Psychical Research (ASPR).[33]

James played a role in America similar to that played by Sidgwick in England. Because of his reputation and manner, he was able to get top people to join the ASPR.

> The original American society included 250 members. They were the cream of the American intellectual life at the time.... By 1890, the American Society was well established and the two groups, American and British, were collaborating closely with each other and with scientists in other countries.[34]

That quotation was taken from an amazing book, *Extraordinary Knowing: Science, Skepticism, and the Inexplicable Powers of the Human Mind*, written by Elizabeth Lloyd Mayer, an internationally known psychoanalyst and clinical psychology professor. Fourteen years prior to starting to work on this book, she had known nothing about the Society for Psychical Research and the whole world of the study of anomalous experiences.

She had stumbled into this world through her search for her daughter's very valuable harp, which had been stolen. Desperate, she took the advice of a friend to find a dowser, because a really good dowser could find not only underground water, the friend said, but "also lost objects." It turned out that the dowser she found, who was the current president of the American Society of Dowsers, was able to tell her that the harp was still in Oakland (where she and her daughter lived). And if she would send an Oakland street map to him in Fayette, Arkansas, he would tell her where it was more particularly. He did. When she got the harp back, she said to herself, "*This changes everything.*"[35]

This realization led to a 15-year quest for understanding. She discovered that "the world of anomalous mind-matter interactions is filled with shoddy research." But what most impressed her was

> the significant bank of well-conducted, scientifically impeccable research that imposes enormous questions on anyone interested in making sense of the world from a Western point of view.[36]

What she most wanted to understand was "why our culture is so fearful about anomalous experiences." And whether it is possible "to investigate apparently anomalous experiences while remaining firmly grounded in rational thought."[37]

For this reason, she was very interested in the work of William James, who "was determined that the American society, like the SPR, its British counterpart, would remain impeccable in adherence to rigorous standards of science."[38]

James's work in psychical research will be discussed in the next chapter and also in Chapter 12.

Whitehead and Psychical Research

Although James himself went part of the way to articulating such a position, the philosopher who most fully developed it was Alfred North Whitehead. Besides expanding James's radical empiricism, with its acceptance of non-sensory perception, Whitehead also developed a full-fledged epistemology that explains the possibility of extrasensory perception.

Whitehead affirmed empiricism. He said: In maintaining that "all knowledge is grounded on perception," philosophy started on a sound principle.[39] But he took issue with *sensationist* empiricism, according to which we perceive only sensory data—"that all perception is by the mediation of our bodily sense-organs, such as eyes, palates, noses, ears, and the diffused bodily organization furnishing touches, aches, and other bodily sensations."[40]

A recent exemplification of sensationism was Harvard philosopher Willard Van Quine (1908–2000), who insisted "that our data regarding the world reach us only through sensory stimulation," adding explicitly that "there is no extrasensory perception."[41]

This sensationist empiricism is based primarily on eighteenth-century philosopher David Hume. Hume concluded from his sensationism that we have no empirical basis for talking about causation, in the sense of the influence of one thing on another. We can only say that there is a *constant conjunction* between certain kinds of events. The one that comes first we call the "cause"; the one that comes second we call the "effect." We don't see any necessary connection between them.

By contrast, Whitehead said that the type of perception on which Hume had focused should be called "perception in the mode of presentational immediacy," because it gives us only data that are immediately present to our conscious experience, such as bright lights, but no information about where those data came from. In Hume's own words,

> the mind [cannot] go beyond what is immediately present to the senses, either to discover the real existence or the [causal] relations of objects.[42]

Hume's position implied, in other words, that you cannot say that the dog you seem to be petting is real; you also cannot say that the apparent dog's biting you was the cause of the pain in your hand. You can say only that you have certain sensory data—colors, shapes, sounds, and tactile feelings. Hume's difficulties arose from the fact that he ignored the fact that we also have "perception in the mode of causal efficacy."

Perception in the Mode of Causal Efficacy

Perception in the mode of causal efficacy is closely related to Whitehead's version of radical empiricism. Like James, Whitehead affirmed the reality of non-sensory perception. Moreover, besides affirming its reality, Whitehead argued that non-sensory perception is fundamental, so that sensory perception is secondary. Far from being primary, sensory perception is derivative from non-sensory perception.

Perception in the mode of presentational immediacy by itself also gives us no knowledge of the real existence of things; it gives us only sensory data. Humean perception, in other words, condemns us to solipsism, according to which we do not know that objects and other people exist.

Philosopher George Santayana, who taught at Harvard just prior to Whitehead's tenure there, extended this Humean argument for solipsism by pointing out that sensory perception also provides no knowledge of the past, so that the sensationist form of empiricism leads to "solipsism of the present moment."[43] In Whitehead's view, we know about time only by means of perception in the mode of causal efficacy[44] and hence by means of non-sensory perception.

One example is our awareness of the fact that sensory data reach us by means of our bodies: We are aware that we see things by our eyes, and we hear things by means of our ears. This perception of the efficacy of our own bodies is a type of non-sensory perception. When we see a star, we are not seeing our eyes; rather, we are aware that we see the star by means of our eyes. This is an example of the fact that non-sensory perception is primary, while sense-perception is secondary.[45]

(Normal perception involves the interplay of causal efficacy and presentational immediacy in what Whitehead called "perception in the mode of symbolic reference." Whitehead said: "When human experience is in question, 'perception' almost always means 'perception in the mixed mode of symbolic reference.'"[46])

Another example of perception in the mode of causal efficacy is memory, in which the mind in a present moment remembers experiences in previous moments. By assuming that the human mind or soul is a single actual entity, most philosophers have not been aware that memory is an example of causation. But Whitehead held an "epochal theory of time," according to which the mind is a temporally ordered society of occasions of experience. Defending the presumption that an actual entity is an act of experience, he said that William James could be quoted in support, when he said: "Your acquaintance with reality grows literally by buds or drops of experience."[47]

Accordingly, there is nothing supernatural about telepathy; one becomes aware of the content of other minds through the same non-sensory mode of perception that tells us about causation, the real existence of physical objects, memory, and time.

We have no evidence that Whitehead, unlike James, devoted any of his time to psychical research. But we have good reason to believe that he was aware of it. When Whitehead was a student at Trinity College, he became in 1884 a member of "the most elite discussion club in the English-speaking university world—the Cambridge Conversazione Society, commonly known as 'The Apostles.'"[48] The nickname "the Apostles" is said to have originated from the fact that when the society was created in 1820, it had twelve members.[49] Whitehead said that the Apostles had "a wonderful influence" on him.[50] He served as the secretary for two years, from February 1885 to February 1887.[51]

Meeting on a Saturday evening, a member read a paper for about twenty minutes on a topic that had been agreed on at the previous meeting and then asked a question raised by the paper. Then everyone voted and could add a comment. One night the question was, "Does the devil exist, or is he merely loathsome?" Whitehead answered, Yes, the devil exists, and then added the comment: "He is the Homogenous."[52]

Anyway, shortly before Whitehead became a member, the society had been led by Henry Sidgwick. In the opinion of Whitehead's biographer, Victor Lowe, Sidgwick had been the "greatest Apostle of the 19th century"—"the perfect incarnation of the wholly dispassionate, uncommitted, but hopeful pursuit of truth."[53] In Whitehead's day, Sidgwick was "still the Apostle par excellence" and still often attended the meetings.[54] Shortly before his death, Sidgwick described the spirit of the Apostles thus:

> *the spirit of the pursuit of truth with absolute devotion and unreservedly by a group of intimate friends, who were perfectly frank with each other and indulged in any amount of humorous sarcasm and playful banter, and yet each respects the other, and when he discourses tries to learn from him and see what he sees. Absolute candor was the only duty that the tradition of the society enforced . . . and there were no propositions so well established that an Apostle had not the right to deny or question, if he did so sincerely and not from mere love of paradox.*[55]

Given the fact that Sidgwick became the president of the Society for Psychical Research, and that this fact, as philosopher C. D. Broad said, gave the SPR "an intellectual and moral status that was invaluable," it would seem that Whitehead would have been predisposed to respect it.

Five: James, Whitehead, and Psychical Research 45

Speaking of Sidgwick, Victor Lowe said, Whitehead "admired the man."[56]

It also seems that this likelihood would have been reinforced by the fact that Broad (whose "basic limiting principles" were discussed earlier) himself was a friend of Whitehead's.[57] Broad had become interested in psychical research as a young man. One of his early books, *Mind and Its Place in Nature*, caused a stir, because it affirmed evidence of psychical phenomena that suggested the possibility of life after death.[58] In the preface to this book, Broad said:

> I shall no doubt be blamed by certain scientists ... for have taken serious account of the alleged facts which are investigated by Psychical Researchers. I am wholly impenitent about this. The scientists in question seem to me to confuse the Author of Nature with the Editor of *Nature*.[59]

In the first chapter of this book, which originated as Tanus Lectures, Broad began by speaking highly of "Dr. Whitehead, who gave the first course" of the Tarner Lectures.[60] (Broad wrote nineteen books. Four of them were on psychical research and/or survival of death.)

But the major fact that would have likely led Whitehead to be favorable to psychical research in later life was his admiration for William James. In Whitehead's first lecture at Harvard, Whitehead said "what an honor it was to be at Harvard—the university of William James."[61] Whitehead later called James "that adorable genius."[62] And in a letter to his one-time assistant Charles Hartshorne, he asked about the biography of James by Ralph Barton Perry, in which Perry had said that James's interest in psychical research was "central and typical." Whitehead asked Hartshorne: "Have you read Ralph Perry's book (2 vols.) on James? It is a wonderful disclosure of the living repercussions of late 19th century thought of a sensitive genius."[63]

Whitehead on Telepathy

Although we do not know that Whitehead devoted any time to psychical research, we do know that he affirmed the reality of telepathy. He understood causation in terms of "feelings" ("positive prehensions"), and telepathy means "feeling at a distance."

As we saw, the second version of the modern worldview was atheistic and materialistic, and so it said that action at a distance not only could not happen naturally, it could not happen period.

Whitehead did not endorse either the first or second versions of the modern worldview. He instead allowed that action at a distance could happen naturally. He did this by means of a distinction between two types of physical prehensions, pure and hybrid.

All physical prehensions objectify previous actual occasions. But actual occasions have two poles, physical and conceptual (or mental). Whitehead explains:

> A pure physical prehension is a prehension whose datum is an antecedent occasion objectified in respect of one of its own *physical* prehensions. A hybrid prehension has as its datum an antecedent occasion objectified in respect of a *conceptual* prehension.[64]

Then Whitehead said:

> There is no reason to assimilate the conditions for hybrid prehensions to those for pure physical prehensions. Indeed the contrary hypothesis is the more natural hypothesis. . . . Thus the doctrine of immediate objectification for the mental poles and of mediate objectification of physical poles seems most consonant to the philosophy of organism in its application to the present cosmic epoch. This conclusion has some empirical support, both from the evidence for peculiar instances of telepathy, and from the instinctive apprehensive of a tone of feeling in ordinary social intercourse.[65]

It does not matter whether one can fully understand Whitehead's reasoning here. The important point, for our purposes, is that he accepted the reality of telepathy. Besides the passage just quoted, he affirmed it in his first American book,[66] one of his last,[67] and in private conversation,[68] and that he was concerned to try to show how his philosophy made it possible.

Edward Kelly on Whitehead

The assessment of Whitehead's importance for psychical research has recently been supported by an outstanding and potentially paradigm-changing book

Five: James, Whitehead, and Psychical Research 47

on psychology entitled *Irreducible Mind: Toward a Psychology for the 21st Century*, based primarily on the work of Frederic Myers, William James, and psychical research. As the title suggests, this book is a critique of materialistic reductionism, showing its many failings. This multi-authored book was written primarily by professors of psychiatric medicine, including the lead author, Edward F. Kelly. In the final chapter, Kelly said that James's unfinished program was "taken up and integrated with emerging developments in physics by the Anglo-American mathematician, philosopher of science, and metaphysician Alfred North Whitehead." Kelly continued:

> [Whitehead's] work in fact represents the most systematic effort to date to elaborate a comprehensive metaphysical system specifically intended to be compatible with both the new basic science and with all available facts of human experience.[69]

Kelly's emphasis on "all available facts of human experience" was central to his appreciation of Whitehead. Kelly, in fact, began the chapter by quoting Whitehead's statement that "rejection of any source of evidence is always a treason to the ultimate rationalism which urges forward science and philosophy alike."[70] Just as Whitehead said that "philosophy can exclude nothing," so that it should start with assemblage,[71] Kelly and his colleagues have applied this method with regard to psychology.

Irreducible Mind is primarily an 800-page rejection of physicalist theories of mind-body relations, according to which the mind can be reduced to the brain. The authors support this rejection by "assembling in one place large amounts of credible evidence for a wide variety of empirical phenomena that appear difficult or impossible to explain in conventional physicalist terms"[72]—phenomena that had been explored by William James and especially James's friend and colleague Frederic Myers, who was the primary intellect behind the founding of the Society for Psychical Research in Britain.

James illustrated the method of "assemblage" that Whitehead recommended. In a passage noted by Kelly, Whitehead said that James was one of the "four great thinkers"—along with Plato, Aristotle, and Leibniz—"whose service to civilized thought rests largely upon their achievements in philosophical assemblage."[73]

Kelly's point was that most philosophers, especially in the late modern world, have failed to assemble all the ideas to which a philosophical position must do justice. Arguably, the experiences to which modern philosophers have most failed to do justice are the experiences on which psychical research has focused. It was this failure that led James to make his previously quoted statement:

> The most urgent intellectual need which I feel at present is that science be built up again in a form in which [the phenomena of psychic research] may have a positive place.[74]

Whether or not it was Whitehead's intention to fulfill this need, it was one of his achievements. This is a major element in the new, postmodern worldview proposed by this book.

This book now turns to psychical research and four examples of its various types of evidence for life after death.

Endnotes

1. Alan Gauld, *The Founders of Psychical Research* (New York: Shocken Books, 1978), 138.
2. Krister Dylan Knapp, *William James: Psychical Research and the Challenge of Modernity* (University of North Carolina, 2017), 108.
3. Knapp, *William James*, 108.
4. C. D. Broad, *Religion, Philosophy and Psychical Research: Selected Essays* ([1953] New York: Humanities Press, 1969), 94.
5. William James, "What Psychical Research Has Accomplished," in *Essays in Psychical Research,* introduced by Robert A. McDermott, in *The Works of William James,* gen. ed. Frederick Burkhardt (Harvard University Press), 90.
6. Deborah Blum, *Ghost Hunters: William James and the Search for Scientific Proof of Life after Death* (New York: Penguin, 2006), 132.
7. Mary B. Hesse, *Forces and Fields: The Concept of Action at a Distance in the History of Physics* (New York: Dover, 2005).
8. Richard J. Westfall, *Never at Rest: A Biography of Isaac Newton* (Cambridge University Press, 1980), 15–16.
9. Westfall, *Never at Rest*, 381.

10. This paragraph was borrowed from my "Parapsychology and Philosophy: A Whiteheadian Postmodern Perspective," *The Journal of the American Society for Psychical Research* (July 1993): 217–88, at 221.
11. This paragraph was modified from my "Parapsychology and Philosophy," 222; the information about Mersenne was taken from R. Lenoble, *Mersenne ou la naissance du méchanisme* (Paris: Librairie Philosophique J. Vrin, 1943).
12. Gordon Baker and Katherine J. Morris, *Descartes' Dualism* (London and New York: Routledge, 1996).
13. William James, *Some Problems of Philosophy* (London: Longmans, Green, 1911), 195.
14. Richard Swinburne, *The Evolution of the Soul* (Oxford: Clarendon, 1986), 198–99.
15. Keith Campbell, *Body and Mind,* 2nd edition (University of Notre Dame Press, 1984).
16. Rachel Laudan, ed., *The Demarcation between Science and Pseudo-Science* (Blacksburg: Center for the Study of Science & Society, 1983); Patrick Grim, ed., *Philosophy of Science and the Occult* (Albany, NY: SUNY Press, 1982).
17. Ray Hyman, *The Elusive Quarry: A Scientific Appraisal of Psychical Research* (Buffalo, NY: Prometheus Books, 1989), 176.
18. James E. Alcock, *Parapsychology: Science or Magic? A Psychological Perspective* (Oxford & New York: Pergamon Press, 1981), 196.
19. Martin Gardner and John Archibald Wheeler, "Quantum Theory and Quack Theory," *New York Review of Books,* 17 May 1979; Richard S. Broughton, *Parapsychology: The Controversial Science* (New York: Ballantine Books, 1991), 75n. Having charged during the AAAS session that J. B. Rhine had falsified an experiment, Wheeler later, learning that his charge was false, wrote a retraction in *Science,* 13 May 1979: 144.
20. Antony Flew, "Parapsychology: Science or Pseudoscience?" in *A Skeptic's Handbook of Parapsychology,* ed. Paul Kurtz (Buffalo, NY: Prometheus Press, 1985), 519–36, at 529.
21. Paul Kurtz, "Is Parapsychology a Science?" in *Paranormal Borderlands of Science,* ed. Kendrick Frazier (Buffalo, NY: Prometheus Books, 1981).

22. George Price, "Science and the Supernatural," in *Philosophy and Parapsychology,* ed. Jan Ludwig (Buffalo, NY: Prometheus Books, 1978), 145–71.
23. Price, "Science and the Supernatural," 152–53.
24. Flew, "Parapsychology: Science or Pseudoscience?" 532.
25. D. O. Hebb, "The Role of Neurological Ideas in Psychology," *Journal of Personality* 20/1 (September 1951): 39–55, at 45.
26. Quoted in Deborah Blum, *Ghost Hunters: William James and the Search for Scientific Proof of Life after Death* (New York: Penguin, 2006), 171.
27. C. D. Broad, *Religion, Philosophy and Psychical Research* (New York: Humanities Press, 1969), 9.
28. Jane Duran, "Philosophical Difficulties with Paranormal Knowledge Claims," in *Philosophy of Science and the Occult,* ed. Patrick Grim (Albany, NY: SUNY Press, 1982), 196–206, at 202.
29. William James, *Essays in Radical Empiricism,* ed. Ralph Barton Perry, published in one volume with James's *A Pluralistic Universe* (New York: E. P. Dutton, 1971), 270–71.
30. *William James on Psychical Research,* ed. Gardner Murphy and Robert O. Ballou (Clifton, NJ: Augustus M. Kelley, 1973), 42.
31. Ralph Barton Perry, *The Thought and Character of William James,* 2 vols. (Boston, Little, Brown, 1935), 155.
32. Robert D. Richardson, *William James: In the Maelstrom of American Modernism: A Biography* (New York: Mariner Books, 2007). The first edition was published by the Houghton Mifflin Company in 2006.
33. Krister Dylan Knapp, *William James: Psychical Research and the Challenge of Modernity* (University of North Carolina Press, 2007), 2.
34. Elizabeth Lloyd Mayer, *Extraordinary Knowing: Science, Skepticism, and the Inexplicable Powers of the Human Mind* (New York: Bantam, 2007), 75.
35. Mayer, *Extraordinary Knowing,* 2–3.
36. Mayer, *Extraordinary Knowing,* 5.
37. Mayer, *Extraordinary Knowing,* 8.
38. Mayer, *Extraordinary Knowing,* 75.

39. Alfred North Whitehead, *Process and Reality: An Essay in Cosmology*, Corrected Edition, ed. David Ray Griffin and Donald W. Sherburne (New York: Free Press), 158.

40. Alfred North Whitehead, *Adventures of Ideas* (New York: Free Press, 1967), 177-78.

41. Lewis Edwin Hahn and Paul Arthur Schilpp, eds., *The Philosophy of W. V. Quine*. Library of Living Philosophers, Vol. 18 (LaSalle, IL: Open Court, 1986), 364; Willard Van Quine, *Theories and Things* (Harvard University Press, 1981), 1–2.

42. David Hume, *A Treatise of Human Nature*, vols. 1 and 2 of *The Philosophical Works of David Hume* (1739), III: II.

43. George Santayana, *Scepticism and Animal Faith* (New York: Dover, [1923] 1955), 14–15.

44. Whitehead, *Symbolism: Its Meaning and Effect* (New York: Macmillan), 1927), 32–35.

45. Whitehead, *Process and Reality*, 168.

46. Whitehead, *Process and Reality*, 168.

47. Whitehead, *Process and Reality*, 68, quoting James, *Some Problems of Philosophy*, Chapter X.

48. Victor Lowe, *Alfred North Whitehead: The Man and His Work*, Vol. I (Baltimore and London: The Johns Hopkins Press, 1985), 112.

49. Wikipedia, "Cambridge Apostles."

50. Lowe, *Alfred North Whitehead*, I: 113.

51. Lowe, *Alfred North Whitehead*, I, 135.

52. Lowe, *Alfred North Whitehead*, I, 136.

53. Lowe, *Alfred North Whitehead*, I, 117.

54. Lowe, *Alfred North Whitehead*, I, 120.

55. Arthur and Eleanor Mildred Sidgwick, *Henry Sidgwick: A Memoir* (London and New York: Macmillan & Co., 1906), 34–35.

56. Lowe, *Alfred North Whitehead*, I: 118.

57. Victor Lowe, *Alfred North Whitehead: The Man and His Work*, Vol. II (Baltimore and London: The Johns Hopkins Press, 1990), 177. Lowe comments only on the fact of their friendship, not also on anything

about psychical research.
58. C. D. Broad, Encycopedia.com.
59. C. D. Broad, *The Mind and its Place in Nature* (London: Kegan, Paul, 1921), viii.
60. Broad, *The Mind and its Place in Nature*, 3–5.
61. Lowe, *Alfred North Whitehead*, II, 141.
62. Whitehead, *Science and the Modern World* ([1925] Free Press, 1967), 2.
63. Lowe, *Alfred North Whitehead:* II, 345–46.
64. Whitehead, *Process and Reality*, 308.
65. Whitehead, *Process and Reality*, 308.
66. Whitehead, *Science and the Modern World*, 150.
67. Whitehead, *Adventures of Ideas*, 248.
68. A. H. Johnson, 1969. "Whitehead as Teacher and Philosopher," *Philosophy and Phenomenological Research* 29 (1969):351–76, at 364.
69. Edward F. Kelly et al., *Irreducible Mind: Toward a Psychology for the 21st Century* (Lanham, MD: Rowman & Littlefield, 2007), 633.
70. Kelly et al., *Irreducible Mind*, 577; quoting Alfred North Whitehead, *The Function of Reason* (1929; Beacon Press, 1968), 61.
71. Alfred North Whitehead, *Modes of Thought* ([1938] Free Press, 1968), 2.
72. Kelly et al., *Irreducible Mind*, 639.
73. Whitehead, *Modes of Thought*, 9, 2.
74. *William James on Psychical Research*, ed. Murphy and Ballou, 42.

CHAPTER SIX

Mrs. Piper and Other Mediums

WILLIAM JAMES MET some of the ounders of the Society for Psychical Research in London shortly after its founding in 1882 "and soon became involved with the society's work." The year of 1884 "saw the launching of the American Society for Psychical Research, in which James was a leading figure." By the middle of 1885, "James was busy attending séances and reporting on [physical] mediums, which he found a 'loathsome occupation.'"[1] (Physical mediums are ones that allegedly produce physical phenomena, such as ectoplasm and the movement of tables.)

But James's attitude to mediumship was changed by his encounter with one mental medium. Most of the attention in the early decades of psychical research was devoted to "mental mediumship," in which a medium, usually in trance, would purportedly put people in touch with departed loved ones and friends.

To believe that mediums can transmit information from deceased individuals, one must accept the reality of telepathy, which is the best-known form of extrasensory perception (ESP). But the modern worldview rules out this possibility, based on the dogma that we cannot perceive anything except by means of our physical senses. James, however, came to reject "the orthodox belief that there can be nothing in anyone's intellect that has not come in through ordinary experiences of sense."[2]

To undermine this belief, James said, we need only one counter-example:

> A universal proposition can be made untrue by a particular instance. If you wish to upset the law that all crows are black, you mustn't seek to show that all that crows are; it is enough to prove one single crow to be white.[3]

"My own white crow," James added, "is Mrs. Piper."[4]

James and Mrs. Piper

James had learned about Leonora Piper from his wife's mother, who was able to learn quite mundane facts from this woman. About her, James wrote:

> My mother-in-law, on her return from Europe, spent a morning vainly seeking for her bankbook. Mrs. Piper, on being asked shortly where this book was, described the place so exactly that it was instantly found.[5]

Although he was skeptical, "James was sufficiently intrigued to go, together with [his wife] Alice, a few days later to see Mrs. Piper for himself. They concealed their names and their connection to his wife's mother."[6] James's wife learned that Mrs. Piper, while in trance, seemed to know almost everything about Mrs. James's kinsfolk. William wrote:

> Some of them were dead, some in California, some in the State of Maine. She characterized them all… spoke of their relations to each other, of their likes and dislikes, of their as yet unpublished practical plans, and hardly ever made a mistake.[7]

Mrs. Piper also described events in the life of William himself. He said, for example: "She told of my killing a gray-and-white cat, with ether, and described how it had 'spun round and round' before dying."[8] (James had begun his career as an assistant professor of physiology at Harvard.)

James remained uncertain that any of Mrs. Piper's apparent communications from spirits of the dead might be genuine, and so his work with her did not convince him of life after death. Indeed, after studying the relevant evidence for 25 years, James said: "I confess that at times I have been tempted to believe that the Creator has intended this department of nature to remain baffling."[9]

However, while being uncertain about life after death, James had no doubts about telepathy. Having made his statement about Mrs. Piper's being his white crow, James explained:

> In the trances of this medium, I cannot resist the conviction that knowledge appears that she has never gained by the ordinary waking use of her eyes and ears and wits. What the source of this knowledge may be we know not, and have not a glimmer of an explanatory suggestion to make; but from admitting the fact of such knowledge I can see no escape.[10]

James thereby, as Krister Knapp put it, "stak[ed] his reputation on Mrs. Leonora Piper."[11] Shortly before his death, James declared:

> Those with the fullest acquaintance of the phenomena admit that in good mediums there is a residuum of knowledge displayed that can only be called supernormal: the medium taps some source of information not open to ordinary people.... I wish to go on record for... the presence, in the midst of all the humbug, of really supernormal knowledge.[12]

Testing Mrs. Piper

After the initial tests of Mrs. Piper by James, the serious testing of her was carried out by Richard Hodgson, an Australian who had come to Boston to be the secretary of the American Society for Psychical Research. Hodgson had a reputation for detecting fraud. For example, he was in 1884 "sent to India where Madame Blavatsky [the co-founder of the Theosophical Society] was currently practicing; Hodgson produced a scathingly negative report on her activities."[13] Hodgson assumed that he would also figure out how Mrs. Piper had been deceiving James and others.[14]

Several facts about Mrs. Piper made her an ideal subject: She was not highly educated, so could not be suspected of being the source of much of the information she conveyed; she was not wealthy (she did not use her gift to get rich), so could not have had a vast number of detectives on her payroll; she was fully cooperative with all the measures imposed by investigators; and she was willing to be investigated for over 25 years.

In spite of Hodgson's confidence that he would expose Mrs. Piper as a fraud, his skepticism was shaken at his first (anonymous) sitting with her, as she in trance conveyed intimate details about his relatives and friends in Australia, which he could see no way she would have known through ordinary means.[15]

Seeing that Mrs. Piper was worthy of further study, Hodgson took great precaution to prevent any possible fraud. To make sure that her apparent trances were authentic, Hodgson

> put ammonia-soaked cloth under her nose, dumped spoonfuls of salt, perfume, and laundry detergent into her mouth, pinched her until she bruised, all without provoking a flinch.[16]

Mrs. Piper and her family were even followed by detectives to make sure they were not making inquiries about people, and letters were checked to guarantee that she was not receiving information from agents. Hodgson admitted: "Mrs. Piper has certainly beaten me."[17] Indeed, she was never, in all the years she was studied, detected doing anything suspicious.[18] James said, "I should be willing to stake as much money on Mrs. Piper's honesty as that of anyone I know."[19]

It cannot be stressed too much how exceptional Mrs. Piper was. Most mediums have been professionals, making money from their work. Richard Hodgson, who devoted much of his time for the SPR to exposing frauds, said that "nearly all professional mediums are a gang of vulgar tricksters."[20] James himself helped discredit some of the professional mediums in Boston. The SPR, looking for talented and honest mediums, found only Mrs. Piper and a very few others.[21]

Leonora Piper herself did not want to be a medium. Expecting a second child, she simply wanted to be a mother and a respectable wife. However, thinking that her talent was a God-given gift, she consented: "She let a friend talk her into sitting with a Boston widow" (Eliza Gibbens, James's mother-in-law).[22]

Six: Mrs. Piper and Other Mediums

As was the case with most mediums, when Mrs. Piper went into trance, a "control" personality would emerge. The meaning of her "control" was explained by Pulitzer-prizewinning science journalist Deborah Blum in her great 2006 book, *Ghost Hunters: William James and the Search for Scientific Proof of Life after Death*.[23] Mrs. Piper's control "served as a kind of spirit business manager, relaying messages, summoning other ghosts into conversations."[24]

Her usual control claimed to be a Frenchman named Dr. Phinuit, who lived from 1790 to 1860, but he was apparently fictitious. (James and his associates could find no evidence that such a man ever existed, and Phinuit could not even speak good French.)[25] In any case, "Shortly after Mrs. Piper went into a trance, her voice would change into his—deep, rough, flavored with a country French accent."[26]

Mrs. Piper, incidentally, said that she did not know what happened when she went into trance. It began, she said, "as if something were passing over my brain making it numb," a sensation similar to being etherized.[27] As to how to explain the psychic phenomena, she was inclined to believe it was based on telepathy, but otherwise she "remain[ed] a student with the rest of the world."[28]

James also had no explanation, saying only that Mrs. Piper had "some exceptional power," but that he had no idea what this power was. Indeed, James said, "the Piper phenomena are the most absolutely baffling thing I know."[29]

One of the baffling things was how irregular her performances were. There were good days and bad days. "Anyone who sat with Mrs. Piper only once, and arrived on one of Phinuit's bad days, was likely to leave disenchanted." But "the transcendental eeriness of the good days could make one forget that."[30]

This irregularity, incidentally, is one of the bases often used by scientific critics to dismiss psychic phenomena. Experimental scientists tend to believe (with apologies to Hegel) that the repeatable is the real and the real is the repeatable. But psychic phenomena, dealing with the human mind rather than atoms and molecules, are never going to have the kind of repeatability that we have with physical and chemical experiments.

Richardson pointed out that James held a middle position, which was neither large nor easy to defend. The spiritualist community. . . looked upon him and the Society for Psychical Research as skeptical debunkers and enemies who unreasonably demanded concrete evidence for everything, while many scientists looked upon him as a gullible spiritualist because he took up such matters at all.[31]

Evidence for Life after Death

Although Mrs. Piper had given what James considered convincing evidence of extrasensory perception, he was less certain, as stated above, as to whether the evidence by her and other good mediums also proved life after death. But sessions with mediums, he had learned, could sometimes be quite impressive.

Sometimes the medium would simply convey what he or she saw and heard from "the other side." But sometimes the deceased individual would seem to speak through the medium's body. Besides giving information evidently known only to the departed and the sitter, or at least not to the medium, the personality might speak with the voice, mannerisms, accent, vocabulary, and intellectual skills of the deceased. The annals of psychical research contain dozens of such cases, in which the personality speaking through the medium seemed to have genuine memories of the life of the person in question.

An example is provided by sittings with Mrs. Piper had by a Reverend and Mrs. Sutton, whose daughter Katherine, nicknamed "Kakie," was the last of three children who had died. The speaker in this session was Phinuit. The words in square brackets are Mrs. Sutton's annotations. Phinuit said:

> A little child is coming to you. . . . Phinuit describes the child and her "lovely curls." Where is Papa? Want Papa. [He (i.e., Phinuit) takes from the table a silver medal.] I want this—want to bite it. [She used to bite it.] . . . . Who is Dodo? [Her name for her brother, George.] . . . Tell Dodo I am happy. Cry for me no more. [Puts hands to throat.] No sore throat any more. [She had pain and distress of the throat and tongue.] . . . . Phinuit said: Here are two more. One, two, three here—one older and one younger than Kakie. [Correct.] Was this little one's tongue very dry? She keeps showing me her tongue. [Her tongue was paralyzed, and she suffered much with it to the end.] Her name

is Katherine. [Correct.] She calls herself Kakie. She passed out last. [Correct.] ... Where is horsey? [I gave him a little horse.] Big horsey, not this little one. [Probably refers to a toy cart-horse she used to like.] Papa, want to go wide [ride] horsey. [She pleaded this all through her illness.][32]

A natural surmise is that Mrs. Piper's subconscious, or alternate personality, was creating "Kakie" out of information being learned telepathically from the Suttons. Although that is plausible, the personality sometimes contradicts the expectations of the sitters, as in this case. In the next sitting, "Kakie," after again asking for the horse and being given the little one, said:

No, that is not the one. The big horse—so big. [Phinuit shows how large.] Eleanor's horse. Eleanor used to put it in Kakie's lap.

Only then did Mrs. Sutton recall the intended horse, which belonged to Kakie's sister Eleanor and was packed away. In a similar misunderstanding, "Kakie" asked for "the little book," meaning a little prayer book that had been given to Kakie just before her death, although Mrs. Sutton at first assumed that she meant a little linen picture book.[33]

On the basis of Mrs. Piper's séances, Hodgson concluded,

after allowing the widest possible margin obtainable ... by ordinary means, by chance coincidence and remarkable guessing, aided by clues given consciously and unconsciously by the sitters, and helped out by the supposed hyperaesthesia on the part of Mrs. Piper,—there remained a large residuum of knowledge displayed in her trance state, which could not be accounted for except on the hypothesis that she had some supernormal power.[34]

The only question is: What kind of supernormal power? On the one hand, it might be the power in trance to receive information from spirits, which is the survivalist hypothesis. On the other hand, it might be an extraordinary degree of power used regularly in trance to bring the results of extrasensory perception and perhaps also psychokinesis with the living to consciousness—the so-called super-psi hypothesis (using the term "psi" for any kind of psychic or paranormal functioning). The super-psi hypothesis is the main alternative to the survival hypothesis.

It would take us beyond the aims of this book to enter into an extensive evaluation of these two options. I can say only that, to my knowledge, the most sophisticated treatment of it is by philosopher Stephen E. Braude in his 2003 book, *Immortal Remains: The Evidence for Life after Death*.[35] Whereas Braude's position is too complex to summarize here, I will say a little: In a section entitled "Survival and the Causal Nexus," he described the world as presented by the super-psi hypothesis as suffering from "crippling complexity." The world's causal nexus contains "an enormously complex web of interactions, psi and nonpsi, overt and covert, local and global."[36] (Although there is no sign that he was influenced by Whitehead, his description of the world's causal nexus is remarkably similar to Whitehead's portrayal of the world of "causal efficacy," in which everything that happens has *some* effect on everything, whether enormous or vanishingly trivial.)

Braude uses a radio analogy, which he usually eschews, on the final page of his book:

> The difference between the causal scenarios posited by the survival and super-psi hypotheses seem akin to the following. The psychic achievement achieved by the super-psi hypothesis resembles tuning a radio to tuning a radio to several different stations, in order to get distinctive collections of information available only from those stations. Each attempt to dial a station and get the needed information can be hampered by drifting signal frequency, multipath distortion, fluctuations in signal strength, or simply making a connection at the wrong time. . . . By contrast, the survivalist scenario resembles an attempt to dial in a single station. Despite inevitable fluctuations in signal strength, the dialer needs only to make that one connection and try to hold onto it. . . . I think we can say, with little assurance but with some justification, that the evidence provides a reasonable basis for believing in personal postmortem survival.[37]

The Cross-Correspondences Case

The annals of psychical research contain dozens of cases of the type described above, in which the personality speaking through the medium seemed to have genuine memories of the life of the person in question. One such case is centered around the so-called "cross-correspondences."

To approach this case, suppose that some psychical researchers were to find themselves still conscious after their bodily deaths, and that they decided to try to devise some system of communications, the results of which would be difficult to explain away by appeal to very strong telepathy. What was required, said a writer named Montague Keen,

> was an experiment which could clearly defeat what was later to become known as the super-psi hypothesis. If it were possible to distribute to more than one medium fragments of messages, in themselves meaningless, and if necessary to provide enough hints to enable a perceptive third party to piece them together to form a coherent message, that would demonstrate the existence of an external intelligence. All the better if the mediums were unknown to one another, living in different parts of the world, and puzzled by the arcane references and obscure language. It would show the final message and the intelligence promoting it, incapable of attribution to any individual medium.[38]

This cross-correspondence project was highly evidential, pointed out Keen, because "it was one thing to show that the memories of deceased persons were somehow accessible to us: quite another to demonstrate that their active intelligences survived after death and could communicate with those left behind."

In the judgment of American philosopher C. J. Ducasse in his book *A Critical Examination of the Belief in a Life after Death*, the cross-correspondences "provide the strongest evidence of 'true' survival."[39] Knapp commented:

> The SPR increasingly believed this method was the most evidential in proving the spirit incarnate, and it dominated the SPR's testing for nearly a quarter of a century, from around 1900 through the early 1920s.[40]

Frederic Myers and Annie Marshall

This case began shortly after the death of Frederic Myers, who, among the founders of the Society for Psychical Research, was the one most intensely interested in the issue of survival. As Deborah Blum explained,

Myers was so interested because a young woman named Annie Marshall had captured his heart, and then died. She had been married to Walter Marshall, a cousin of Myers. Annie had been desperately unhappy for several years, partly because Walter had become mentally ill. After he became so violent that he had to be institutionalized, Myers's mother offered Annie a place to live.

Myers himself, who had become friends with Annie, attended a few séances with her,[41] searched for a doctor for Walter, and otherwise tried to help her. In the process, he fell in love with her, but resolved not to let her know, so as not to complicate her life while she was still in shock. Myers told his diary that he preferred "irredeemable woe to the slightest shadow of wrong."[42]

After Walter was locked away, Annie, who blamed herself for their failed marriage and for her role in his institutionalizing, fell apart and committed suicide. Blum added: "[Myers] was wrenched with feelings of guilt and inadequacy. He began to believe that he must talk to Annie again—for both their sakes."[43]

Myers spent much of the rest of his life searching for proof of life after death and trying to contact Annie. He did not, however, find the results of these first attempts satisfactory. It is possible, however, that he continued his efforts after he died.

Shortly after Myers's death, Mrs. Margaret Verrall, a classics scholar who was very fond of Myers, decided to take up automatic writing in the hopes of enabling him to demonstrate his survival of death. After some months, she received a simple message in Greek and Latin, both of which she knew. The message was signed "Myers."[44]

The message would have seemed meaningless, except that Rector, another of Mrs. Piper's spirit guides, began reporting messages from Myers. Mrs. Verrall's daughter, Helen, then joined in, as did nine more friends of Myers. Soon there were twelve widely separated women, some of whom were not in contact with each other,[45] who began writing scripts of messages they had purportedly received from Myers.

These women included (in addition to Mrs. Piper, Margaret Verrall, and her daughter Helen), Mrs. Coombe-Tennant (the first British delegate to the League of Nations), and Alice Kipling Fleming in India (a sister of Rudyard Kipling). The scripts are called the cross-correspondences because topics, words, and phrases referred to in one script would commonly be mentioned in one or more other scripts at about the same time.

For example, Mrs. Fleming, working in India, produced a script saying "Maurice. Morris. Mors [the Latin word for death]. The script by Mrs. Piper included "Sanatos" and "Sanatos." A few days later, her script had "Thanatos" [which is the word for death in Greek, which Mrs. Piper did not know]. A few days later, "Thanatos" appeared three times.[46]

Most of the messages did not make sense until two or three scripts were combined. And yet the scripts, after being produced, were simply filed away. It was several years before anyone had an inkling about the correspondences. It was suggested to Mrs. Piper's "Myers" that "he" should indicate when a cross-correspondence is being attempted by drawing a circle with a triangle in it.[47]

After some delay, a message came through that Myers was being assisted in the communications by Richard Hodgson, who had worked extensively with Mrs. Piper and had died in 1905. Soon after, Mrs. Verrall's "Myers" wrote: "an anagram would be better. Tell him that—rats, star, tars, and so on." While living, Hodgson had been addicted to anagrams, and a list of these very anagrams was found among his papers. The following week, Mrs. Verrall's "Myers" wrote "Aster" [Greek for "Star"] and "Teras" [wonder], followed by quotations from Robert Browning. These quotations began with, "The world's wonder." This was followed by a triangle within a circle.[48]

A few days later, the "Myers" personality, coming through Helen Verrall, drew a monogram, a star, and a crescent. Mrs. Verrall then wrote: "A monogram, the crescent moon, remember that, and the star." In a couple more weeks, Mrs. Piper's "Myers" asked if Mrs. Verrall had received the name "Evelyn Hope" [the title of one of Browning's poems]. "Myers" then added: "I also said . . . look out for Hope, Star, and Browning." A few days later, Helen Verrall's "Myers" drew a star and wrote:

> That was the sign she will understand when she sees it. . . . No arts available . . . and a star above it all rats everywhere in Hamelin town [Browning, of course, had written a poem on the Pied Piper of Hamelin].[49]

This is merely a tiny portion of the cross-correspondences. There were some 3,000 scripts, and they contained many allusions, especially the scripts purportedly from Myers, that were in Latin and Greek. A serious attempt to evaluate the correspondences for evidence of life after death would require a fuller study, such as that provided by H. F. Saltmarsh in *Evidence for Personal Survival from Cross-Correspondences*.[50] But the above paragraphs should provide a glimpse of the nature of the project.

Many people, of course, would prefer a non-survivalist interpretation of the scripts. But providing one would not be easy. Some people may be tempted to dismiss the correspondences as mere coincidences. But this sort of thing continued for 30 years, and sometimes the references to the other scripts were much more direct. "Myers," for example, would sometimes tell one of the automatists what "he" had written in the script of another.[51]

More plausible than coincidence would be the super-ESP hypothesis, expanded to the super-psi hypothesis to allow for telepathic influence (psychokinesis) from one automaticist to others.[52]

Such an attempt would naturally begin with the scripts of Mrs. Verrall, whose work began the case. However, the cross-correspondences continued for sixteen years after her death. It appears that, if the scheme for the cross-correspondences was planned by a group of discarnate clever souls to make the super-psi hypothesis difficult, they did a good job.

That is, one could suppose that Mrs. Verrall, who knew Latin, Greek, and the classics and who was the first to begin receiving scripts, created her own scripts through her own knowledge combined with the dramatic powers of her unconscious, then induced the scripts in Mrs. Piper in Boston, Mrs. Fleming in India, and the other nine women through unconscious telepathic influence, all the while monitoring all the scripts through unconscious clairvoyance to keep the pattern of response and counter-response up to date.

One problem with this view—apart from its enormous complexity—is that Mrs. Verrall (and her daughter Helen) had no prior knowledge of three of the seven communicators. Also, in some of the cross-correspondences, her own scripts were not involved, so the correspondences had to be created without anyone knowing either Greek of Latin. Finally, the episode continued for sixteen years after her death, so one of the other automaticists, none of whom knew the classics and the languages nearly as well as Mrs. Verrall, would have had to assume her role.

A caveat: Citing messages that seemed to come through clearly can give the impression that it was easy for "Myers" and the other communicators to get their messages through quite easily. But this evidently was not the case. After explaining why "he" chose the Browning poem, "Myers" added that "he" had more to say, but it was so incredibly frustrating getting the smallest shred of thought across.[53] Indeed, some the messages of "Myers" seethed with frustration:

> Yet another attempt to run the blockade—to strive to get a message through.... The nearest simile I can find to express the difficulties of sending a message is that I appear to be standing behind a sheet of frosted glass—which blurs sight and deadens sound—dictating freely—to a reluctant and somewhat obtuse secretary.[54]

After Henry Sidgwick died, his wife, Eleanor ("Nora") Sidgwick—the principal of Newnham College and the SPR's best editor and statistician[55]—continued to work on the cross-correspondences project. After working on it for seven years, she concluded: "The cross correspondence studies offered real evidence of cooperation by friends and fellow-workers no longer in the body."[56]

Conclusion

This chapter shows that there is no doubt that telepathy occurs. James said: "The concrete evidence for most of the 'psychic' phenomena under discussion is good enough to hang a man 20 times over."[57]

This chapter also shows that mediums have sometimes provided fairly clear and accurate information. This was especially the case with Leonora Piper, but one should not think that she was the only one. For example, the ability of British medium Gladys Osborne Leonard (1882–1968) was reportedly comparable to that of Mrs. Piper, as was Rosina Thompson, the wife of a London merchant, who "produced the kind of results previously only seen with Leonora Piper."[58] Mrs. Thompson's control was reputedly a child, her daughter Nelly, who had died some years before.

In a letter to James in 1899, Myers said that his first sittings with Mrs. Thompson had been unremarkable.

But one day little Nelly announced the approach of a spirit almost as bright as God—brighter & higher, at any rate, than any spirit whom she had thus far seen. That spirit with great difficulty descended into possession of the sensitive's organism—& spoke words which left no doubt of her identity.... He [Myers] could almost hear Annie Marshall calling him.[59]

Mrs. Thompson wrote down "a promise that Myers would be reunited with his long-dead Annie—and soon."[60] "Annie Marshall" became a control; James and others called her the "A-Control." Her behavior was carefully documented by Myers in sittings with Mss. Piper and Thompson.[61]

In any case, the most important feature of the cross-correspondences case is how it contrasts with a central weakness of most mediumistic messages: that they seem to reflect earlier concerns of the purported communicators. By contrast, the cross-correspondences seem to reflect contemporary, sustained purposes better than did other mediumistic messages.

Endnotes

1. Robert D. Richardson, *William James: In the Maelstrom of American Modernism: A Biography* (New York: Mariner Books, 2007), 259.
2. William James, "What Psychical Research Has Accomplished," in *Essays in Psychical Research,* Introduction by Robert A. McDermott (Harvard University Press, 1986).
3. Gardner Murphy and Robert O. Ballou, eds., *William James on Psychical Research* (Clifton, NJ: Augustus M. Kelley, 1973), 40–41.
4. Murphy and Ballou, *William James on Psychical Research,* 40–41.
5. Murphy and Ballou, *William James on Psychical Research,* 40–41.
6. Richardson, *William James,* 258.
7. William James, "Address to the President before the Society for Psychical Research" (1896), in James, *Essays in Psychical Research* (Cambridge: Harvard University Press, 1986), 127–37, at 131.
8. James, "Address to the President," 108–10.
9. James, "Address to the President," 108–10.

Six: Mrs. Piper and Other Mediums

10. James, "Address to the President," 84.
11. Krister Dylan Knapp, *William James: Psychical Research and the Challenge of Modernity* (University of North Carolina Press), 113.
12. William James, *Essays in Psychical Research*, 372.
13. Richardson, *William James*, 259.
14. Alan Gauld, *Mediumship and Survival: A Century of Investigations* (London: Granada, 1983), 253.
15. Gauld, *Mediumship and Survival*, 253.
16. Deborah Blum, *Ghost Hunters: William James and the Search for Scientific Proof of Life after Death* (New York: Penguin, 2006), 181.
17. Blum, *Ghost Hunters*, 166.
18. Gauld, *Mediumship and Survival*, 256.
19. Blum, *Ghost Hunters*, 161.
20. Blum, *Ghost Hunters*, 117.
21. Blum, *Ghost Hunters*, 119.
22. Blum, *Ghost Hunters*, 98.
23. Blum, *Ghost Hunters*, 134.
24. Blum, *Ghost Hunters*, 134.
25. Blum, *Ghost Hunters*, 134.
26. Blum, *Ghost Hunters*, 134.
27. Blum, *Ghost Hunters*, 181.
28. Blum, *Ghost Hunters*, 254.
29. Blum, *Ghost Hunters*, 223.
30. Blum, *Ghost Hunters*, 164.
31. Richardson, *William James*, 263.
32. Gauld, *Mediumship and Survival*, 40–42.
33. Gauld, *Mediumship and Survival*, 40–42.
34. Richard Hodgson, "A Further Record of Observations of Certain Phenomena of Trance," *Proceedings of the Society for Psychical Research* 13 (1898): 284-582, at 285.
35. Stephen E. Braude, *Immortal Remains: The Evidence for Life after Death*

(Rowman and Littlefield, 2003), 11–23, 37–38, 73–74, 86–95.

36. Braude, *Immortal Remains*, 86–87.
37. Braude, *Immortal Remains*, 306.
38. Montague Keen, "Cross-Correspondences: A Brief Introduction."
39. C. J. Ducasse, *A Critical Examination of the Belief in a Life After Death*, second edition (Springfield, IL: Charles C. Thomas, 1961).
40. Knapp, *William James*, 253.
41. "Frederic W. H. Myers," Psi Encyclopedia, by the Society for Psychical Research, London.
42. Blum, *Ghost Hunters*, 68.
43. Blum, *Ghost Hunters*, 68–69.
44. Blum, *Ghost Hunters*, 276.
45. Blum, *Ghost Hunters*, 276.
46. Knapp, *William James*, 209.
47. Knapp, *William James*, 310.
48. Knapp, *William James*, 310.
49. Blum, *Ghost Hunters*, 279.
50. H. F. Saltmarsh, *Evidence for Personal Survival from Cross-Correspondences* (London: G. Bell and Sons, 1938).
51. See, for example, a summary of the famous "Hope, Star and Browning" case in Gauld, *Mediumship and Survival*, 81–83.
52. Blum, *Ghost Hunters*, 279.
53. Blum, *Ghost Hunters*, 280.
54. Blum, *Ghost Hunters*, 285.
55. Blum, *Ghost Hunters*, 177.
56. Blum, *Ghost Hunters*, 319.
57. Blum, *Ghost Hunters*, 213.
58. Blum, *Ghost Hunters*, 234.
59. Blum, *Ghost Hunters*, 235.
60. Blum, *Ghost Hunters*, 235.
61. Blum, *Ghost Hunters*, 253.

CHAPTER SEVEN

Near-Death Out-of-Body Experiences

Another kind of evidence for life after death can be provided by the study of out-of-body experiences (OBEs). There are two major types of OBEs: (1) ones that come about in ordinary circumstances; and (2) ones that come about when people are physically near death, called near-death out-of-body experiences (ND OBEs).

Near-Death Out-of-Body Experiences

Near-death experiences (NDEs) typically have two phases: a mundane phase, in which one is experiencing this-worldly things, such as the patient's hospital room, followed by a transcendental phase, in which one has otherworldly experiences, such as going through a tunnel, moving up towards a bright light, seeing deceased relatives, experiencing a life review, and being told to go back to his or her body. (This transcendental phase is often referred to simply as a NDE, whether or not it is preceded by a mundane OBE.)

The term "out-of-body experience" is a phenomenological description, not necessarily also an ontological claim. That is, to say that some people had out-of-body experiences is to say that they had experiences in which they seemed to themselves to be out of their bodies.[1] An OBE is simply "an experience in which a person seems to perceive the world from a location outside his [or her] body."[2] Whether people's minds or souls are literally outside their bodies is at the center of the critical discussion of these experiences.

The view that one's mind is really outside the body is the "extrasomatic" hypothesis. The view that one's soul or mind remains in the body is known as the "intrasomatic" hypothesis. The critical question is: Which hypothesis can better account for the various features of OBEs?

Materialists necessarily endorse the intrasomatic view, because the extrasomatic hypothesis, as materialistic philosopher Susan Blackmore put it, violates the materialistic view that all "mental phenomena depend upon, or are an aspect of, brain events."[3]

The present chapter deals entirely with the mundane phase of near-death OBEs, which occur entirely in "this world," usually primarily in the vicinity of the person's body. These experiences may provide evidence that a person is really out of his or her body. If OBEs are truly experiences had while being out of the body (the "extrasomatic" interpretation), then they imply a radical challenge to modern assumptions about the relation of perception and thought to the brain.

But is there any good reason to adopt the extrasomatic interpretation for some OBEs? Several medical doctors have written books about ND OBEs that have put forward this interpretation, such as Dr. Raymond Moody's 1975 groundbreaking book, *Life after Life*.[4] But the dominant tendency in the medical community and other scientific circles has been to assume the correctness of some version of the intrasomatic hypothesis, according to which the feeling of being outside the body is an illusion.

This opinion, however, is based primarily on the assumption that some such theory *must* be true, because extrasomatic experiences are taken to be impossible. One medical doctor, Dr. Richard Blacher, explaining why he accepted the intrasomatic interpretation of all OBEs,[5] said that the only alternative would be

> one of something (the soul?) leaving the person in reality and hovering over the table. I do not think one has to apologize for

scientific belief if one does not accept the idea of spirits wandering around the emergency room.[6]

Some theories, for example, propose that OBEs result from things related to a near-death situation, such as painkilling drugs, the fear of death, a shortage of oxygen in the brain, or an excess of carbon dioxide in the brain. However, not all OBEs are near-death related, and even in those that are, one of the posited conditions is sometimes not present.

Another theory, building on the fact that most OBErs report very pleasant emotions and an absence of pain, attributes the experience to a release of endorphins. But an endorphin injection results in a loss of pain for 20 to 70 hours, whereas OBE experiencers report that their pain returns the moment they seem to reenter their bodies.[7]

Two other obvious suggestions are that the OBErs are dreaming or having schizoid hallucinations. Physiological studies, however, show that the bodily state during OBEs is not similar to the dream state.[8] And, besides the fact that personality inventories reveal no similarities between OBErs and the mentally ill, psychotic hallucinations tend to be primarily auditory and otherwise to differ greatly from person to person, whereas OBEs are primarily visual and are remarkably consistent from person to person.[9]

In addition to the feeling of being out of one's body, other common features of OBEs are: (1) A strong conviction that the experience is real; (2) normal or better-than-normal hearing; (3) normal or better-than-normal visual perception; and (4) an exceptionally positive emotional state.[10]

However, these features cannot be used for definitely preferring the extrasomatic hypothesis, because advocates of the intrasomatic hypothesis can just dismiss all of these features as fantasies. But OBEs sometimes have another feature, which does support the extrasomatic hypothesis.

Veridical OBEs: Discussion

When people have OBEs, they afterwards are sometimes able to report events they had no normal way of knowing about that can be corroborated by others. This is especially the case with regard to ND OBEs, given the typical circumstances.

For example, one who has a near-death OBE is typically on a hospital bed after having a heart attack. The OBE occurs when one is not breathing, one's heart is not beating, and one's eyes are closed and may even be taped shut. Nevertheless, a person may later report having heard and seen the doctor and nurses working on him or her. If the person's reported perceptions are corroborated by one of the doctors or nurses or some other reliable witness, researchers speak of veridical perceptions.

Persons normally cannot see without receiving visual information from their eyes. Of course, we have visual experiences in dreams, without receiving information from our eyes. But such visual experiences do not constitute "seeing" unless they provide us with accurate information about the world beyond our minds.

Reports of veridical perceptions during OBEs have serious implications for the mind-body relation. Accordingly, some scholars interested in the possibility of life after bodily death have become very interested in the study of OBEs with veridical perceptions.

To be sure, OBEs are fascinating even apart from the issue of veridical perceptions. Having an OBE often leads one who had the experience to conclude that his or her mind can exist apart from the body. And ND OBEs, whether or not they are preceded by a mundane OBE, often contain transcendental experiences that seem utterly real. Persons who have had these experiences often take them as foretastes of their life after death. Moreover, Kenneth Ring, one of the giants of NDE studies, reported that

> the NDE tends to bring about lasting changes in personal values and beliefs—[people who have these experiences] appreciate life more fully, experience increased feelings of self-worth, have a more compassionate regard for others and indeed for all life, develop a heightened ecological sensitivity, and report a decrease in purely materialistic and self-seeking values. Their religious orientation tends to change, too, and becomes more universalistic, inclusive and spiritual in its expression. In most instances, moreover, the fear of death is completely extinguished.[11]

Nevertheless, neither transcendental near-death experiences, nor mundane OBEs without veridical perceptions, can be taken as evidence that the experiences were extrasomatic, certainly not evidence that can be considered scientific: Both types of experience can simply be dismissed as fantasies, hallucinations.

An article entitled "The Science of Near-Death Experiences," published in the *Atlantic* in 2015, explained why scientists have increasingly become interested in near-death experiences:

> Many NDEs happen when a person is surrounded by an arsenal of devices designed to measure every single thing about the body that human ingenuity has made us capable of measuring.... As medical technology continues to improve, it's bringing people back from ever closer to the brink of death. A small, lucky handful of people have made full or nearly full recoveries after spending hours with no breath or pulse, buried in snow or submerged in very cold water.... All of this makes NDEs perhaps the only spiritual experience that we have a chance of investigating in a truly thorough, scientific way.[12]

Although this statement refers simply to NDEs, the author, Gideon Lichfield, clearly meant near-death *out-of-body experiences*, as he added:

> As the only stage in an NDE that involves perceiving the physical rather than the spiritual world, an out-of-body experience has the most potential to convince skeptics.[13]

To emphasize this point: Reports of NDEs and OBEs simply cannot be seriously presented as evidence for anything, or even as unquestionably authentic, unless they contain veridical perceptions.

For example, a medical doctor named Eben Alexander published a bestselling book entitled *Proof of Heaven: A Neurosurgeon's Journey into the Afterlife*.[14] The book, which reportedly recounted near-death experiences Alexander had while in a coma, made him rich and famous. But it also led to seemingly interminable debates, with some writers seeking to debunk his account and others seeking to defend it by debunking the debunkers. Because Alexander's book provides no reports of veridical perceptions, there is simply no good way for the supporters of Alexander's book to refute the debunkers.

Veridical ND OBEs: Seven Examples

A most remarkable feature of OBEs—whether they occurred in ordinary circumstances or as the mundane phases of NDEs—is that their perceptions are remarkably accurate. In a chapter of *The Handbook of Near-Death Experiences* (2009), Janice Miner Holden wrote:

> Of the 111 cases of apparently nonphysical perception [in near-death experiences that I studied], I found that 92 percent contained absolutely no errors, 6 percent contained minor errors, and only 2 percent were completely erroneous. Thus, the vast majority of these apparently nonphysical perceptions were veridical.[15]

Given this introduction, the rest of this section looks at seven examples of people who had ND OBEs with veridical perceptions. Veridical perceptions in ND OBEs provide evidence (albeit not proof) that life after physical death is possible. The strongest reason to doubt this claim involves the appeal to super-psi: the argument that the veridical perceptions in OBEs can be equally explained by regarding them as "imagery-rich manifestations of ESP"—that is, of super-telepathy combined with super-clairvoyance.[16] I ask readers to evaluate this alternative hypothesis in reading these seven cases.

Holly

I begin with the story with which psychiatrist Bruce Greyson began his 2021 book *After,* a book about near-death experiences, some of which included veridical OBEs, one of which is the incident that got him started on his 45-year scientific study of NDEs.

Greyson described an incident in which he got tomato sauce on his tie just before interviewing the roommate of a female student named Holly, who was unconscious in a hospital room from trying to commit suicide by taking an overdose of drugs. He interviewed the roommate, Susan, in a family lounge, far away from Holly's room. The next day, after changing his clothes, he interviewed Holly, who promptly told him that she saw him talking with Susan. Greyson said: "There was no way she could have seen or heard us talking at the far end of the corridor." Holly, insisting emphatically that she *saw* him, said: "You were wearing a striped tie that had a red stain on it." Greyson enlarged on how unbelievable he found the incident: "She then went on to repeat the conversation I'd had with Susan, all my questions and Susan's answers. . . , without making any mistakes."[17]

Young Dr. Greyson thought "that there must be some reasonable physical explanation for how Holly knew these things. . . . The only alternative was that the part of Holly that thinks and sees and hears and remembers somehow left her body and followed me down the hall to the family lounge and, without benefit of eyes or ears, took in my conversation with Susan. That made no sense to me at all. I couldn't even imagine what it would mean to leave my body. As far as I could tell, I *was* my body."[18]

But years later, when he had become the director of the psychiatric service at the University of Virginia, Raymond Moody, whose *Life after Life* had become a surprise bestseller, came to ask Greyson, who was his training supervisor, for help in responding to all the letters Moody received. Greyson was stunned to learn "that Holly's experience, which had knocked me for a loop, was not at all unique."[19]

The more Greyson learned about NDEs, "the more they seemed to cry out for an explanation beyond the limited understanding of our everyday ideas about the mind and the brain. And those new ways of thinking of our minds and our brains open up the possibility of exploring whether our consciousness might continue after the death of our bodies."[20]

Greyson said "accurate vision from an out-of-body viewpoint doesn't happen very often in NDEs,"[21] but it has clearly happened in enough cases not to be ignored. It led Grayson to say, in a chapter entitled "A New View of Reality," that his study of NDEs led him

> to appreciate that some of the things I'd been taught about the mind and the brain were assumptions rather than facts. The idea that our minds—our thoughts, feelings, hopes, fears—are produced solely by our brains is not a scientific fact. It is a philosophical theory proposed to explain scientific facts.[22]

His way of putting the issue may be better than posing it as the question whether the mind is literally outside the body. Greyson says:

> Experiences like NDEs seem to me to involve both the physical brain and the nonphysical mind [see Appendix II on the way a Whiteheadian would understand this distinction].... Although our physical brain and nonphysical mind seem to work as one unit in everyday life, people who have had NDEs consistently say that their experience of being awake and aware while their brains are impaired convinces them that their minds can act independently of their brains at times.[23]

I find the most important thing about Greyson's revised outlook is its recognition that we need "a new view of reality."

He also supports this book's position on the importance of veridical ND OBEs. In a discussion about how to tell the difference between real and fake NDEs, Greyson said: "I don't know how to test the validity of stories about otherworldly realms. But I *can* test the reports of seeing things in our physical world."[24]

Maria

When a migrant worker named Maria was visiting friends in Seattle in 1977, she had a heart attack. She was rushed to Harborview Hospital and placed in the coronary care unit. A few days later, she had a cardiac arrest, from which she was resuscitated rather quickly. The following day, she was visited by her critical care social worker, Kimberly Clark, a professor at the University of Washington's School of Medicine.

Anxious to tell Clark "the strangest thing," Maria told her that during her cardiac arrest, she was able to look down from the ceiling and watch the medical team working on her body. At one point in this experience, Maria said, she found herself outside the hospital, where she spotted a blue tennis shoe on the ledge of the north side of the third floor. Maria added that one of its laces was stuck underneath the heel and that the little toe area was worn. Wanting to know whether she had actually seen that shoe, she begged Clark to try to locate it, and Clark, who years before had herself had an NDE,[25] agreed. Describing her effort, Kimberly Clark said:

> I went up to the third floor and began going in and out of the patients' rooms and looking out their windows, which were so narrow I had to press my face to the screen just to see the ledge at

Seven/Near-Death Out-of-Body Experiences

all. Finally, I found a room where I pressed my face to the glass and looked down and saw the tennis shoe!

Having retrieved the shoe, Clark confirmed Maria's observations about the shoelace and the worn little toe area. "The only way she could have had such a perspective," Clark said, "was if she had been floating right outside."[26] The shoe, she said, "was very concrete evidence for me."[27]

Al Sullivan

On 18 January 1988, a 56-year-old van driver named Al Sullivan had emergency quadruple bypass surgery at Hartford Hospital in Connecticut. After being given an anesthetic, he had an NDE, with both mundane and also transcendental experiences (in which he saw his deceased brother and mother). After regaining consciousness, he told his cardiologist, Dr. Anthony LaSala, about his mundane experience. While observing his body in the operating room from above, he reported, he saw the cardiac surgeon, Dr. Hiroyoshi Takata, flapping his elbows as if he were trying to fly. Realizing that Sullivan's experiences were not simply based on the drugs he had been given, Dr. LaSala explained that this was a peculiar habit of Dr. Takata's.[28]

In 1997, Dr. Bruce Greyson (one of the authors of this account) spoke with Drs. LaSala and Takata. Dr. Takata confirmed that what Sullivan called "flapping" was a regular practice: After he has scrubbed in, he does not wish his hands to touch anything until he is actually ready to do the surgery, so he flattens his palms against his chest and gives instructions to his assistants by pointing with his elbows. Dr. LaSala added that he had never seen any other surgeons using their elbows like this.[29]

When Greyson asked Sullivan if he remembered any more details about what he had observed, Sullivan said that he had seen Dr. Takata standing alone over his opened chest, which was being held open by metal clamps. He also saw two other surgeons working over one of his legs. He was puzzled why they were working on a leg when his heart was the problem. Sullivan later learned that the surgeons were stripping the vein out of his leg to create the bypass graft for his heart.[30]

The article in which Greyson (along with two colleagues) gave this account was published in 1998. In his 2021 book, *After*, Greyson added that the detail about stripping the vein:

clearly established that Al [Sullivan] had been completely unconscious when he'd witnessed the cardiac surgeon flapping his arms. He couldn't possibly have seen that bizarre behavior with his eyes because his brain was fully anesthetized and his eyes were taped shut—something that is often done to keep patients' eyes from drying out.... He shouldn't have been able to see anything. And yet he did.[31]

Pam Reynolds

The story about Maria has long been the best-known example of veridical perception in ND OBEs; close behind is now the account of singer-songwriter Pam Reynolds, who in 1991, at age 35, underwent surgery to remove an aneurysm at the base of her brain. If it were to burst, it would kill her; but the standard surgery to drain and repair it might also kill her. So her surgeon—in a procedure known as "hypothermic cardiac arrest"—chilled her body to 60 degrees F., which stopped her heart, and then drained the blood from her head. (The cooling would prevent her cells from dying while deprived of oxygen.)[32]

After Pam's eyes were lubricated and then taped shut, the surgeon—in order to make certain that her brain was completely inactive during the operation—had her ears fitted with small speakers that made continuous clicks at 100 decibels. If any part of her mind was working, the clicking would cause electrical signals in the brain stem.[33] The surgeon, Dr. Robert Spetzler, then began cutting through Pam's skull with a Midas Rex bone saw, which produces a noise similar to a dental drill.

Following the surgery, Pam said that, after the surgeon had begun cutting her skull, she felt herself "pop" out of her body and hover above it, watching as doctors worked on her body. She was able to report several details about what had happened.

Saying that she hated the dental-drill sound of the bone saw, she said that the saw "looked like an electric toothbrush"—an accurate description of a Midas Rex bone saw.

When a female cardiac surgeon was attempting to locate the femoral artery in Pam's right groin, Pam heard a male voice saying, "Try the other side." She also heard a female voice say, "We have a problem. Her arteries are too small."[34]

Finally, Pam reported hearing the song "Hotel California" (by the Eagles), to which the staff was listening.[35]

After the operation, and before any of her perceptions had been shown to be veridical, Pam assumed she had been hallucinating. But a year later, she told some of her experiences to Dr. Spetzler.

Spetzler did not check out the details, but this task was performed by cardiologist Michael Sabom, who wanted to put NDEs on a professional footing.[36] His 1981 book, *Recollections of Death*,[37] started the study of veridical perceptions in near-death experiences. In any case, the records from Pam's surgery, reported Sabom, matched her memories, including the conversation about her arteries, the electric-toothbrush-appearing bone saw, and the playing of "Hotel California."[38]

57-Year-Old Man

In 2014, a multi-hospital project known as AWARE studied the awareness of 140 patients who had survived cardiac arrest. The study, led by Dr. Sam Parnia of Stony Brook University, focused on the accuracy of reports of visual and auditory perception during cardiac arrest. Especially noteworthy was the account of a 57-year-old man who had had an ND OBE.[39] According to a summary of the patient's statements:

> He felt quite euphoric during the experience.
>
> The patient heard an automated voice saying "Shock the patient, shock the patient."
>
> The patient said: "I was on the ceiling looking down. I saw a [male] nurse that I did not know beforehand who I saw after the event. I could see my body and saw everything at once. I saw my blood pressure being taken whilst the doctor was putting something down my throat. I saw a [nurse] pumping on my chest."
>
> The patient also said that there was a man—bald and "quite a chunky fella"—who wore blue scrubs and a blue hat. ("I could tell he didn't have any hair, because of where the hat was.")
>
> The next day, the patient recognized the bald man, who had attended him during the resuscitation.

The medical record confirmed the use of an Automated External Defibrillator, which would give the automated instructions the patient heard and the role that the identified man played during the resuscitation.[40]

Dr. Parnia told the *Independent*: "The man described everything that had happened in the room, but importantly, he heard two bleeps from a machine that makes a noise at three minute intervals. So we could time how long the experience lasted for."

This patient's testimony changed the opinion of the doctor, who "previously thought that patients who described near-death experiences were only relating hallucinatory events."[41]

44-Year-Old Man

In 2001, *The Lancet*, a highly respected medical journal, published a large study of NDEs directed by Dr. Pim van Lommel of Rijnstate Hospital in the Netherlands. The study included 344 survivors of cardiac arrest from 10 hospitals, 18 percent of whom reported having had an NDE.[42]

One of the patients was a 44-year-old man, who had arrived at the hospital in a comatose state. When the (male) nurse attempted to resuscitate the patient, the nurse found the patient was wearing dentures, which he removed and placed in the patient's cart. A week later, when the man regained consciousness, this nurse came to his room to administer drugs. Upon seeing him, the man exclaimed:

> Oh, yes, but you know where my dentures are. Yes, you were there when they brought me into the hospital, and you took the dentures out of my mouth and put them into that cart. It had all these bottles on it, and there was a sliding drawer underneath, and you put my teeth there.[43]

The nurse and the staff learned that the man had had an OBE. He said that during it, he watched his resuscitation, trying to make those present aware that he was still alive, so that they should keep trying to save him. Dr. van Lommel wrote: "The facts of the case were later verified down to the descriptions the man gave of the doctors and nurses present at the time."[44]

ND OBEs of the Blind: Vicki Umipeg

As researchers became increasingly aware of OBEs and NDEs, they began wondering whether blind persons ever have them and, if so, whether they differ from the experiences of sighted people. Having found that blind persons do have NDEs and OBEs, Kenneth Ring and Sharon Cooper carried out a study of 31 such persons, 21 of whom had had ND OBEs and 10 of whom had had OBEs without being near death.

Another question was whether the NDEs and OBEs of people who had been blind from birth were different from those who had been able to see in the past. Ring and Cooper found that they did not substantially differ. The only difference was that those who were blind from birth did not have visual perceptions in their dreams.[45]

Here is an example provided by Ring and Cooper. Having been born prematurely, weighing only 3 pounds, Vicki Umipeg was born blind, because an excess of oxygen in the incubator had destroyed her optic nerve. When Vicki was 22, she was working as a singer at a nightclub in Seattle. One night, she couldn't get a taxi after work, so she accepted a ride from some patrons, who turned out to be intoxicated. The car crashed, and she suffered serious injuries, including a fractured skull.

After she was taken to a room in Harborview Hospital, she felt that she had left her body and floated up toward the ceiling. She heard a male doctor talking about the possibility that damage to her eardrum could make her deaf as well.

Looking down, she saw a body, at first not being certain it was hers (she, of course, had never seen her own body). But then she realized it was, because she recognized her wedding ring, which was very distinctive, and her hair, which was very long; she was upset that some of it had been shaved off. She also saw that her head was cut, and there was a lot of blood (although she could not tell that it was red, because thus far she had no concept of color).

She then "went up through the roof"; it seemed like the roof had "just melted." She then started feeling a tremendous sense of freedom, which gave her joy. "It was wonderful to be out there and be free, to not worry about bumping into anything." She then had a rather classic transcendental NDE, which she found overwhelming, but she was soon told that she had to go back to take care of her children. When she returned to her body, she said, "It was excruciatingly painful."[46]

These seven cases illustrate the fact that people who are clinically dead can have experiences, sometimes veridical ones at that. For materialists this is impossible, so, as neuroscientist Mario Beauregard said in *The Spiritual Brain*, they simply ignore the evidence.[47] As an example, Harvard cognitive scientist Steven Pinker said that, "when the physiological activity of the brain ceases, as well as anyone can tell the person's consciousness goes out of existence."[48] In speaking of "anyone," Pinker evidently ignored the testimony of doctors, nurses, and professors like those in these seven accounts.

Another example: Neal Grossman, emeritus professor of philosophy of the University of Illinois at Chicago, asked a materialist what it would take to convince him, short of having an NDE himself, that NDEs are genuine. The man replied:

> Even if I were to have a near-death experience myself, I could conclude that I was hallucinating, rather than believe that my mind can exist independently of my brain.[49]

Veridical OBEs and Life after Death

The modern denial of life after death is based primarily on two claims: (1) life after death is impossible, because there can be no conscious experience without information from a functioning brain; and (2) even if one thought that life after physical death might be possible, there could be no good evidence for it. For example, the feeling in OBErs that they are really out of their body proves nothing, because OBEs can be understood as intrasomatic.

However, if OBEs include veridical perceptions, they show that the experiencers have seen and/or heard things that suggest that their minds or souls were really, as they seemed to be, outside their bodies. Visual near-death OBEs of people who have been blind from birth show that minds or souls can have visual perceptions that are not derived from the brain.

The previous chapter, on mediums, shows at the least that extrasensory perception, especially telepathy, occurs. This point undermines one of the bases for claiming that there can be no life beyond physical death. The evidence in this chapter also provides good evidence, even if not quite proof, that people can continue to have experiences after their brains no longer provide sensory data.

OBEs greatly increase the evidence for life after death beyond that which is provided by mediums. The crucial issue here is the occurrence of veridical OBEs, in which claims made by people during these experiences are corroborated by doctors or other credible witnesses. Materialists have to dismiss the significance of OBEs by calling them purely subjective phantasies or hallucinations, but veridical OBEs show that reports from OBEs can have objectivity. Materialists cannot even use the super-psi way of explaining away evidence, because they do not accept psi of any type. Veridical OBEs do not prove the reality of life after death, but they do undermine a main argument for calling it impossible. As psychiatrist Bruce Greyson said,

> If it is true that minds can function in extreme circumstances without physical brains, then it may be possible that minds can continue to exist after the death of the brain.[50]

Endnotes

1. Glen O. Gabbard and Stuart W. Twemlow, *With the Eyes of the Mind: An Empirical Analysis of Out-of-Body States* (New York: Praeger, 1984), 138.
2. Susan J. Blackmore, *Beyond the Body: An Investigation of the Out-of-the-Body Experience* ([1982] Academy Chicago Publishers, 1992), 1.
3. Susan J. Blackmore, *Dying to Live* (New York: Harper Collins, 1993), 47.
4. Dr. Raymond A. Moody, Jr., *Life after Life* (New York: Bantam, 1975).
5. Richard S. Blacher, "Commentary: To Sleep, Perchance to Dream...," *Journal of the American Medical Association* 242. 21 (23 November 1979), 2291.
6. Blacher, "Near-Death Experiences" (letter), *Journal of the American Medical Association* 244.1 (4 July, 1980): 30.
7. Michael Sabom, *Recollections of Death: A Medical Investigation* (New York: Harper & Row, 1982), 171–72.
8. Blackmore, *Beyond the Body*, 125–31.
9. Harvey J. Irwin, *Flight of Mind: A Psychological Study of the Out-of-Body*

Experience (Metuchen, NJ: Scarecrow 1985), 245.

10. Emilio Tiberi, "Extrasomatic Emotions," *Journal of Near-Death Studies* 11/3 (Spring 1993), 149–70, at 158; Sabom, *Recollections of Death,* 28; Blackmore, *Beyond the Body,* 68, 93.
11. Kenneth Ring and Evelyn Elsaesser Valarino, *Lessons from the Light* (Needham, MA: Moment Point Press, 2006), 2–3.
12. Gideon Lichfield, "The Science of Near-Death Experiences," *Atlantic,* April 2015.
13. Lichfield, "The Science of Near-Death Experiences".
14. Eben Alexander, *Proof of Heaven: A Neurosurgeon's Journey into the Afterlife* (New York: Simon & Schuster, 2012).
15. Janice Miner Holden, "Veridical Perception in Near-Death Experiences," in *The Handbook of Near-Death Experiences: Thirty Years of Investigation,* ed. Janice Miner Holden, Bruce Greyson, and Debbie James, 2nd Printing (Westport, CT: Praeger, 2009).
16. Stephen E. Braude, *Immortal Remains: The Evidence for Life after Death* (Lanham, MD: Rowman and Littlefield, 2003), 253.
17. Bruce Greyson, *After: A Doctor Explores What Near-Death Experiences Reveal about Life and Beyond* (New York: St. Martin's Essentials, 2003), 5.
18. Greyson, *After,* 8.
19. Greyson, *After,* 9.
20. Greyson, *After,* 10.
21. Greyson, *After,* 68.
22. Greyson, *After,* 209.
23. Greyson, *After,* 209, 211.
24. Greyson, *After,* 94.
25. Kimberly Clark Sharp, *After the Life: What I Discovered on the Other Side of Life Can Change Your World* (New York: William Morrow, 1995).
26. Kimberly Clark, "Clinical Interventions with Near-Death Experiences," in *The Near-Death Experience: Problems, Prospects, Perspectives,* ed. Bruce Greyson and Charles P. Flynn (Springfield, IL: Charles C.

Thomas, 1982), 242–55, at 242–43.

27. Mario Beauregard, "Near Death, Explained," Salon, 21 April 2012.
28. Emily Williams Cook, Bruce Greyson, and Ian Stevenson, "Do Any Near-Death Experiences Provide Evidence for the Survival of Human Personality after Death?" *Journal of Scientific Exploration*, 12/3 (1998).
29. Cook, Greyson, and Stevenson, "Do Any Near-Death Experiences Provide Evidence?"
30. Cook, Greyson, and Stevenson, "Do Any Near-Death Experiences Provide Evidence?"
31. Greyson, *After,* 68.
32. Lichfield, "The Science of Near-Death Experiences."
33. Beauregard, "Near Death, Explained."
34. Beauregard, "Near Death, Explained."
35. Lichfield, "The Science of Near-Death Experiences."
36. Mario Beauregard and Denyse O'Leary, *The Spiritual Brain: A Neuroscientist's Case for the Existence of the Soul* (New York: HarperCollins, 2007), 158.
37. Sabom, *Recollections of Death.*
38. Barbara Bradley Hagerty, "Decoding The Mystery of Near-Death Experiences," NPR, 22 May 2009.
39. Sam Parnia et al., "AWARE—AWAreness during REsuscitation: A Prospective Study," *Resuscitation* (journal), 2014.
40. Parnia et al., "AWARE—AWAreness during REsuscitation."
41. Adam Withnail, "Life after Death? Largest-Ever Study Provides Evidence that 'Out of Body' and 'Near-Death' Experiences May Be Real," *Independent,* 7 October 2014.
42. Graham Nichols, "Near Death and Out-of-Body Experiences: In Search of the Truth—Noetic Now," Blog, 9 August 2016.
43. Nichols, "Near Death and Out-of-Body Experiences."
44. Nichols, "Near Death and Out-of-Body Experiences."
45. Kenneth Ring and Sharon Cooper, "Near-Death and Out-of-Body Experiences in the Blind: A Study of Apparent Eyeless Vision," *Journal of Near-Death Studies,* December 1997.

46. Ring and Cooper, "Near-Death and Out-of-Body Experiences in the Blind." For more on experiences of the blind, see Kenneth Ring and Sharon Cooper, *Mindsight: Near-Death and Out-of-Body Experiences in the Blind,* 2nd ed. (Bloomington, IN: iUniverse: 2008).
47. Beauregard and O'Leary, *The Spiritual Brain,* xii.
48. Quoted in Beauregard and O'Leary, *The Spiritual Brain,* xv.
49. Quoted in Beauregard and O'Leary, *The Spiritual Brain,* 166.
50. Greyson, *After,* 221.

CHAPTER EIGHT

Apparitions

Another type of evidence for life after death consists of apparitions, in which an individual (usually deceased or dying) briefly appears visually to one or more people. The person who appears is known as "the apparent." This was the first type of evidence that was systematically studied by the Society for Psychical Research, which was carried out primarily in the late nineteenth and early twentieth centuries.

The dominant modern view about apparitions is that they can all be dismissed as pathological hallucinations. This dismissal, however, is ill-informed, partly for the reason that the two phenomena are quite different: Unlike the hallucinations of the insane, apparitions are not correlated with illness or morbidity. In addition, apparitions are primarily visual, whereas (pathological) hallucinations are primarily auditory. Moreover, most people who have seen one apparition never see another.[1]

History of the Study of Apparitions

Apparitions were originally called "phantasms." The first major study was *Phantasms of the Living*, written primarily by Edward Gurney.[2] Its main purpose was to provide evidence for telepathy, which occurred whenever the apparition was "veridical," providing information that the percipient(s) had no way of knowing by normal means.

It turned out that some of the veridical apparitional cases seemed to provide evidence for life after death. This was because the term "living" in Gurney's title, "Phantasms of the Living," was defined liberally: apparitions were counted as living if they occurred within twelve hours of the person's death. Gurney justified this extension on the basis of his theory of "telepathic deferment," according to which the information received telepathically might not rise to consciousness in the form of an apparition until several hours later, when the subject was in a more receptive state of mind.[3]

A few years later, Eleanor Sidgwick—the wife of Henry Sidgwick, the first president of the Society for Psychical Research—was the primary author of a publication called "Report on the Census of Hallucinations." Its purpose was to show that it was very unlikely that most of the apparitions that closely coincided with the death of the apparent could be explained in terms of chance. In other words, there is usually a causal connection between the death and the apparition. Later studies showed that about 60 percent of apparitions occur within an hour of the apparent's death.[4]

A third major study of apparitions was a large section, "Phantasms of the Dead," in Frederic Myers's posthumous two-volume masterpiece, *Human Personality and Its Survival of Bodily Death* (1903).[5]

However, serious studies of apparitions by members of the Society for Psychical Research did not continue, partly because the members felt that they had learned all they were going to learn about apparitions, and partly because, thanks to the discovery of Mrs. Piper, mental mediumship became the Society's primary focus of attention. As a result, when George Tyrrell gave a lecture in 1942, which turned into his book *Apparitions*, he drew largely on the material assembled by Frederic Myers and Eleanor Sidgwick.

The fact that the material in Tyrrell's book was old does not mean that it was unreliable, because the standards for acceptance by the Society for Psychical Research were very strict.

Since that time, there have not been a lot of new reports. However, polls show that apparitions continue to occur at about the same frequency, and there have been a few more recently researched reports about apparitions.[6] One of these was a 1995 article entitled "Six Modern Apparitional Experiences," written by Ian Stevenson[7] (whose writings are central to the chapter on reincarnation below). One of Stevenson's cases will be examined below.

Kinds of Apparitions

It is important to know the kinds of apparitions that have occurred in order to evaluate the pathological hallucination hypothesis. One important classification involves the status of the "apparent" (the person who appears), namely, whether at the time of the apparition the apparent is living, dead, or dying. One important fact is that apparitions of the dying constitute a majority of the recorded apparitions, with evidently about 60 percent occurring within an hour of the apparent's death. Another important fact is that there is no difference, phenomenologically, between apparitions of the living, on the one hand, and those of the dying and long dead, on the other.[8]

But the most important distinction is between apparitions that are "veridical"—ones in which the person(s) who saw the apparition acquired true information that would not have been knowable by normal means—and those that are not.

Veridical Apparitions

The most decisive evidence against the idea that all apparitions are pathological hallucinations is provided by the existence of veridical apparitions. There are well-documented cases, for example, in which apparitions of people who had died revealed to members of their family where they had hidden money or an important document.

One example was about a farmer in Iowa named Michael Conley, who in 1891 died in an outhouse at a place he was visiting in Dubuque. The coroner replaced Conway's clothes, which were covered in filth from the outhouse, with black clothes and a white shirt, plus felt slippers. On learning about Conley's death, one of his daughters fell into a swoon. When she awoke, she asked:

> Where are father's clothes? He has just appeared to me dressed in a white shirt, black clothes, and felt slippers, and told me that after leaving home he sewed a large roll of bills inside his gray shirt with a piece of my red dress, and the money is still there.[9]

Although the family figured that she had simply had a hallucination, her brother telephoned the morgue, found that the father's clothes were still there, and arranged to fetch them. After the son told the coroner what his sister had said, the coroner reported that she was right about the burial clothes, including the felt slippers. They then found the roll of bills in the grey shirt sewed in with a piece of red cloth.[10]

Multiple Apparitions

In an even more common kind of veridical apparition, information is given about how the apparent was injured or killed. The claim that all apparitions are pathological hallucinations is even less persuasive in relation to multiple and collective apparitions. In a multiple apparition, two or more persons at different locations see the apparition within roughly the same time period.

One story involves Eldred Bowyer-Bower, an airman who was shot down over France on the morning of March 19, 1917. That same day, his half-sister, who was in Calcutta, India, and did not know that he was in combat, had a surprising sighting. She reported:

> At the time I was either sewing or talking to my baby.... The baby was on the bed. I had a very strong feeling that I must turn round; on doing so I saw my brother, Eldred W. Bowyer-Bower. Thinking he was alive..., I was simply delighted to see him, and turned around quickly to put baby in a safe place on the bed, so that I could go on talking to my brother; then turned again and put my hand out to him, when I found that he was not there. I thought he was only joking, so I called him and looked everywhere. It was only when I could not find him I became very frightened and the awful fear that he might be dead.... Two weeks later I saw in the paper he was missing.[11]

Eldred also had a sister in England. The same day as the first sister saw him, he was also seen by the three-year-old daughter of this second sister. The daughter came into her mother's bed room and announced: "Uncle Alley Boy is downstairs."

Incidentally, the very fact that it occurred so many decades ago, before communication was so rapid between England and Calcutta, made it easier to be certain that the apparition was discussed before any word of the apparent's fate could have been known through normal channels.

Finally, nine months later, an apparition of Eldred was seen by his fiancée and his mother.[12]

Collective Apparitions

In a collective apparition, two or more persons see it simultaneously at the same place. They see the apparition's "frequent adaptive reaction to the physical situation . . . ; they may recede from persons present and walk around physical obstructions." And, as Tyrell pointed out, in collective apparitions "the several percipients seem to observe the same apparitional figure each according to his position and distance from the figure."[13] Stevenson commented: "These features suggest to me, rather strongly I must say, that some directing personality animates the perceived apparition."[14]

Collective apparitions, as Stevenson pointed out, "provide an important difficulty for persons who do not favor interpreting any of the cases as affording evidence for survival." In a longer statement, Stevenson wrote:

> Collective apparitions occur less often than the simpler types of case that lend themselves more easily to the interpretation of telepathy between living persons. These exceptional cases are, nevertheless, sufficiently numerous and (some of them) sufficiently well authenticated so that the proponent of the telepathic hypothesis of apparition is obliged either to ignore them altogether or to account for them by what appear to me to be improbable secondary explanations.[15]

Psychic Contagion Hypothesis

However, there is one way for these opponents of the survivalist interpretation to escape, this being the idea of "psychic contagion." According to this idea, one person—let's say, a woman with two sisters—hallucinates an image of her deceased mother and then induces it telepathically to her sisters in the room.

But this hypothesis faces insuperable difficulties. One is the problem of spatial perspective: All the percipients see an apparition in the same place and from their own perspective, so that, for example, one sister may see it from the back, another from the front, a third from the left side. How could a percipient see a hallucination from one perspective and then induce it telepathically in other percipients from different perspectives?

There is also a temporal problem. Sometimes an apparition will fade in, remain a while, and then fade out, and yet everyone seeing it agrees on when it became visible and when it faded away. An ability to induce visions with such sophistication and precision would go far beyond any demonstrated ability to induce images telepathically in other people.

Finally, it has been claimed that collective apparitions are so rare that they can be dismissed as anomalies or hoaxes. However, studies have shown that, when two or more persons are present, apparitions tend to be collective from one-third to one-half of the time.[16]

Agency by the Apparent

The cumulative weight of the evidence, accordingly, favors the view that apparitions are sometimes produced in part by some agency beyond that of the percipient(s). Forbidding dogma aside, the natural supposition would be that the apparition was caused, at least in part, by the agency of the apparent himself or herself. Stephen Braude judged that "the best of these cases . . . pose a clear problem for the super-psi hypothesis."[17]

Why Not More Veridical Apparitions?

One further point about the phenomenology of apparitions is relevant to their evidentiary nature with regard to life after death. A common objection to using apparitions to support belief in life after death is that, if this capacity to appear and perhaps even speak and bring about physical effects, really existed, we should expect much more evidence of this sort than we have. Most people who lose friends and loved ones evidentially receive no sign.

However, while the ability to perceive, especially visually, in the out-of-body state is reportedly often as good as normal, the ability to bring about physical effects is evidently extremely rare. This difficulty in producing physical effects is consistent with the fact that, although a few apparitions are able to speak, most of them do not; in fact, some of them reportedly seem to be trying to speak but cannot. Most of them, moreover, produce no physical effects at all.[18]

It is quite possible, accordingly, that the reason most souls do not put in an appearance after separation from their bodies is that they are unable to do so.

An Ian Stevenson Case

One of Stevenson's reported apparitions occurred in 1975. A Scottish woman, known as E. W. in the report, lived across the street from Ronald McKay, who was the manager of a nearby factory, and Betty, his wife. E. W. knew that they had gone on vacation in England, 150 miles from their home. One morning, nevertheless, E. W. saw Ronald walking out of the driveway of his house and then along the road toward his factory. Ronald was wearing a nylon shirt tucked into flannel trousers, his customary work clothes. E. W. remarked to her husband that she was surprised to see that the McKays were already back home.

A half hour or so later, a senior employee of the factory came by and told E. W.'s husband that Ronald McKay had died while on vacation in England—that Ronald had died in his sleep about 7:00 that morning. Stevenson said that the interval between Ronald's death and the apparition seen by E. W. could at most have been three to four hours.[19]

Quasi-Physical Features of Apparitions

Apparitions can behave very strangely. Although they can seem physical, they can also behave in ways that no physical object can behave. So scholars sometimes speak of apparitions as quasi-physical. Stevenson explained why:

> They may appear and disappear without "coming and going" like ordinary persons or objects; they may pass through solid walls and closed, locked doors; and they may move about by gliding instead of walking. Yet apparitions (or at least some of them) also behave in certain respects like ordinary persons and objects.... For example, apparitions may be reflected in mirrors.[20]

Veridical Apparitions and Veridical OBEs

Evidence for life after death is strengthened by taking veridical apparitions and veridical OBEs together, because what is an apparition from one perspective may be an OBE from another. This was the main point of a study of apparitions by Hornell Hart in 1956. He argued that veridical OBEs "provide an internal view of the phenomena observed externally in connection with apparitions of the living." He then marshaled data to show that knowledge about the living acquired in OBEs "are in most respects essentially indistinguishable from apparitions of the [dead and] dying."[21]

If Hart was right, then the appearances of Jesus reported in the New Testament, insofar as they were authentic, could be taken as out-of-body experiences of Jesus.

Could the Appearances of Jesus Be Understood as Apparitions?

Traditional Christian New Testament scholars and theologians have treated the "resurrection of Jesus" as a miracle, meaning that it was different in kind from all other events (except for other miracles).

However, some prominent New Testament scholars, while accepting the historicity of the resurrection, have disagreed with the view that it was absolutely unique. This disagreement involves a difference in how the event called "the resurrection of Jesus" is understood. Those who speak of the uniqueness of this event usually think in terms of the "bodily resurrection of Jesus Christ." But some other New Testament scholars think in terms of analogies with modern-day apparitions. They speak of "the appearances of Jesus after his death"—as did St. Paul, who wrote nothing about an empty tomb.

For example, in 1907, Kirsopp Lake, who taught at the universities of Leiden and Harvard, published a book entitled *The Historical Evidence for the Resurrection of Jesus Christ*, in which he said: "The phenomenon which we call the Resurrection cannot be isolated, but must be considered in connection with others which belong to the same class."[22]

Likewise, B. H. Streeter, professor of biblical exegesis at Oxford University and a member of the Archbishop's Commission on Doctrine in the Church of England, published a book in 1912 entitled *Foundations: A Statement of Christian Belief in Terms of Modern Thought*. Streeter said that the resurrection appearances to the disciples were visions "directly caused by the Lord himself, veritably alive and personally in communication with them."[23] A few years later, Streeter published a book entitled

Immortality: An Essay in Discovery Coordinating Scientific, Psychical, and Biblical Research.[24]

Similarly, C. J. Cadoux, professor of church history at Oxford University, said in a 1941 book that the appearances were

> real manifestations given to his followers by Jesus himself, not by means of his physical body resuscitated from the empty tomb, but by way of those strange processes sufficiently attested to us by psychical research, but as yet very imperfectly understood.[25]

To give a more recent example: In a 2007 book about Jesus, the late professor Marcus Borg of Oregon State University pointed out that St. Paul, who gave the first accounts in the New Testament about the resurrection, reported that Jesus *appeared* to various people—a term that is often used in the Bible in connection with apparitions understood as paranormal experiences, not visible to everybody. "An apparition does not involve a physical body," explained Borg, "even though what is seen often includes seeing a person in bodily form."[26] That Paul thought of the resurrection appearances as apparitions, Borg continued, "is further suggested by his inclusion of himself in the list of people to whom the risen Christ appeared," which implied that Paul "regards his own experience of the risen Christ [his vision on the Damascus Road] as similar to the others." Borg added that "visions and apparitions can be true," so we need "not put them in the category of [pathological] hallucinations."[27] In other words, the resurrection appearances could be categorized as veridical apparitions.

Endnotes

1. George Tyrrell, *Apparitions* (New Hyde Park, NY: University Books, 1961), 22.
2. Edmund Gurney, F. W. H. Myers, & Frank Podmore, *Phantasms of the Living,* two volumes (Cambridge University Press, 1886).
3. Tyrrell, *Apparitions,* 44.
4. Carl B. Becker, *Paranormal Experience and Survival of Death* (Albany, NY: SUNY Press, 1993), 51; Karlis Osis and Erlendur Haraldsson, *At the Hour of Death* (New York: Avon, 1977).

5. Frederic W. H. Myers, *Human Personality and Its Survival of Bodily Death,* in 2 volumes (Longmans, Green, & Co., 1903).
6. Ian Stevenson, "The Contribution of Apparitions to the Evidence for Survival," *Journal of the American Society for Psychical Research* 76.4 (1982): 341–58.
7. Ian Stevenson, "Six Modern Apparitional Experiences," *Journal of Scientific Exploration* 9.3 (1995).
8. Becker, *Paranormal Experience,* 51.
9. Frederic W. H. Myers, *Human Personality and Its Survival of Death* (1903), ed. and abridged into a one-volume edition by Susy Smith (New Hyde Park, NY: University Books, 1961), 228–29.
10. Myers, *Human Personality,* 228–29.
11. Myers, *Human Personality,* 230–31.
12. Myers, *Human Personality,* 139, 230–31.
13. Tyrrell, *Apparitions,* 72.
14. Ian Stevenson, "The Contribution of Apparitions."
15. Stevenson, "The Contribution of Apparitions."
16. Alan Gauld, *Mediumship and Survival* (Academy Chicago, 1984), 240.
17. Stephen E. Braude, *Immortal Remains: The Evidence for Life after Death* (Lanham, MD: Rowman and Littlefield, 2003), 227.
18. Tyrrell, *Apparitions,* 63, 77–80; Becker, *Paranormal Experience,* 47.
19. Stevenson, "Six Modern Apparitional Experiences," Case 4.
20. Stevenson, "The Contribution of Apparitions."
21. Hornell Hart, "Six Theories about Apparitions," *Proceedings of the Society for Psychical Research* 50 (May 1956): 153–239, at 177, 235.
22. Kirsopp Lake, *The Historical Evidence for the Resurrection of Jesus Christ* (London: Williams and Norgate, 1907).
23. B. H. Streeter, *Foundations: A Statement of Christian Belief in Terms of Modern Thought* (New York: Macmillan, 1912), 136.
24. B. H. Streeter, *Immortality: An Essay in Discovery Coordinating Scientific Psychical and Biblical Research* (New York: Macmillan, 1921).
25. C. J. Cadoux, *The Historic Mission of Jesus* (Lutterworth Library, UK:

1941), 166.

26. Marcus J. Borg and N. T. Wright, *The Meaning of Jesus: Two Visions,* 2nd ed. (New York: HarperOne, 2007), 132–33.

27. Borg and Wright, *The Meaning of Jesus,* 132–33.

CHAPTER NINE

Reincarnation

THE IDEA of reincarnation has been extremely controversial, even a subject of ridicule, in the West, even though it has been accepted throughout most of the rest of the world. Philosopher Arthur Schopenhauer (1788–1860) suggested, only half jokingly, that the European world (including Canada, the United States, and Australasia) could be defined as that part of the world that rejects reincarnation.[1]

Reincarnation and Christianity

This rejection has, to a significant extent, been due to the fact that reincarnation has widely been considered inconsistent with Christianity, according to which one's everlasting destiny is determined by one lifetime on Earth.[2] Hebrews 9:27 has been widely used as a proof-text: "It is appointed for men to die once, and after this comes judgment."

Conservative Christian theologians almost universally reject reincarnation as heretical. For example, German theologian Helmut Thielicke included reincarnationist teaching among a list of "blasphemous" theories of immortality.[3] Thielicke evidently believed that this judgment was justified by a ecclesiastical condemnation of it in the Middle Ages.

However, although the church has officially frowned on reincarnationism, it has, according to Cardinal Mercier, "never been formally condemned by the Roman Catholic Church."[4]

Some early Christian theologians even endorsed reincarnation, including Justin Martyr and probably Origen. A group called the pre-existiani, who taught a transmigrationist type of doctrine, was by no means looked upon with the disfavor that adherence to such views later evoked. According to philosopher and Episcopal priest Geddes MacGregor, who long taught religion at the University of Southern California,

> Origen certainly taught a doctrine of the pre-soul and probably taught a form of reincarnationism, and his influence, as the greatest thinker of his day in the Christian Church, was immense.[5]

However, there were several factors that conspired to prevent official acceptance of the doctrine of reincarnation, and these factors have led to the widespread view that the doctrine is irrevocably opposed to Christian faith. This negative view was expressed by Catholic thinker Thomas Ryan in the title of a 2015 article, "25 percent of US Christians believe in reincarnation. What's wrong with this picture?" Ryan said:

> According to data released by the Pew Forum on Religion and Public Life (2009 survey), not only do a quarter of Americans believe in reincarnation, but 24 percent of American *Christians* expressed a belief in reincarnation. This represents a significant deviation from the traditional Judaeo-Christian narrative with which most Americans in the baby-boomer generation grew up. You were born. You lived. You died. And after a judgment you went to heaven or hell forever.[6]

The traditional isolation of European and North American Christians from people who accepted reincarnation had also meant a lack of exposure to people who believe in it. Recently, however, with the decline of supernaturalist Christianity, the growing adoption of Hindu and Buddhist spiritualities, and serious studies of the grounds for reincarnation, the belief in it has been growing rapidly. (As a bumper sticker puts it, "Reincarnation is making a comeback.")

Nevertheless, prejudice against the idea remains strong in many circles. Some of the grounds for hostility are based on the mistaken assumption that all believers in reincarnation accept the retributive idea of karma, which, as usually understood in the West, implies that the unfortunate are simply getting what they deserve from a past life—a belief that can rationalize passivity in the face of suffering and injustice. However, most cultures that accept reincarnation do not accept this understanding of karma.[7]

Another unwarranted assumption is the idea that, if reincarnation is true for some souls, it must be true for all. However, the strongest conclusion warranted by the evidence is that reincarnation is a form that life after death sometimes takes, and the "sometimes" could well mean "only occasionally": In the parts of the world that encourage the reporting of memories of past lives, reports of such memories are made only by one child in 1,000 or, in a few places, one in 500.[8] Jim Tucker, in a book entitled *Life before Life,* said that "we must remember that what is true about the children who report past-life memories may not be true for the rest of us."[9]

But the main reason to reject or ignore even the best evidence for occasional reincarnation is the fact that "scientific materialism is the largely unquestioned basis for modern science's understanding of life" and that "the materialist perspective has essentially become the modern educated position."[10]

The Work of Ian Stevenson

The development of better understandings of reincarnation has been due primarily to the work of one scholar, Ian Stevenson, who taught psychiatry at the University of Virginia.

Providing dozens of "cases of the reincarnation type" (Stevenson's term), Stevenson almost single-handedly changed the status of such cases in the parapsychological community. At one time, this community largely ignored the issue of reincarnation, putting the discussion of it at the end of books on life after death. But after Stevenson's work became well known, books about evidence for life after death started putting the discussions of reincarnation at the beginning, treating it as the strongest type of evidence.[11]

In a typical case, a child between the ages of 2 and 4 begins talking about an earlier life, usually giving the name of the person the child believed he or she had been. The child also usually gives the names of other members of the family and of the place where the former person lived. The child would also typically plead with its parents to take it to see its "real" family.

In such cases, the person who seemed to have been reincarnated is likely to be someone who died young, often violently, from 4 months to 4 years prior to the birth of the child in question. If the prior person died violently, the child may have a phobia corresponding to the cause of death. If the prior personality spoke a different language, the child may have a remarkable facility for that language.[12]

If possible, Stevenson would carry out interviews before the two sets of parents had met, so that he could record the child's statements to check for accuracy. The potentially verifiable statements usually turned out to be 80–90% correct.

Stevenson's studies were so meticulous that some mainstream scientists were impressed.

> The physicist Doris Kuhlmann-Wilsdorf—whose groundbreaking theories on surface physics earned her the prestigious Heyn Medal from the German Society for Material Sciences, surmised that Stevenson's work had established that 'the statistical probability that reincarnation does in fact occur is so overwhelming . . . that cumulatively the evidence is not inferior to that for most if not all branches of science.'"[13]

Jesse Bering, who had always written from a materialist perspective, said:

> When you actually read [the best cases] firsthand, many are exceedingly difficult to explain away by rational, non-paranormal means. . . . Why do we wonder where our mind goes when the body is dead? Shouldn't it be obvious that the mind is dead too? Perhaps it's not so obvious at all. I'm not *quite* ready to say that I've changed my mind about the afterlife. But I can say that a fair assessment and a careful reading of Stevenson's work has, rather miraculously, managed to pry it open. Well, a *tad*, anyway.[14]

With regard to best attempts to explain the cases away, Stephen Braude said: "These pose a clear problem for the super-psi hypothesis."[15]

Some Cases

Here are a few of the best typical cases, with "best" meaning that they are veridical, in the sense that researchers have identified the person whose life the child remembered. The one exception in this list is Ma Tin Aung Myo.

Imad Elewar

The case that Stevenson considered his best involved a boy named Imad Elewar, who was born in Lebanon in 1958 to a family belonging to the Druze religion, an Islamic sect that accepts reincarnation.[16] Before Imad was 2 years old, virtually as soon as he could talk, he began speaking of a former life, which turned out to correspond to that of one Ibrahim Bouhamzy, a playboy who had lived in a village about 25 miles away and had died in 1949 of tuberculosis at the age of 25.

Stevenson arrived in Imad's village in 1964, when Imad was five and a half. Through conversations with Imad and his parents, Stevenson was able to write down 57 potentially verifiable details about Imad's recollections before there had been any contact between the Elewar and the Bouhamzy families. At the end of Stevenson's investigation, 51 of these statements had been confirmed. There were many facts indicating that Imad's life was in some sense a continuation of Ibrahim's.

One type of such facts was that Imad knew about Ibrahim's life. Imad knew the name of Ibrahim's mistress, "Jamileh" (a pseudonym), and the fact that she wore high heels (which was uncommon for Druze women in small villages in those days).

Imad knew that Ibrahim, who loved to hunt, had a rifle and double-barreled shotgun, and even knew in which closet the rifle (which was illegal) was hidden.

He knew that Ibrahim had a yellow car, a truck for hauling rocks, a sheep, a goat with a kid, and a brown dog who was held by a cord (not a chain, as was common).

Imad knew the name of Ibrahim's sister (Huda) and the brother to whom he was closest (Fuad). Imad also knew Ibrahim's last words: "Huda, call Fuad."

Also significant were several people and events that Imad recognized: When the families of Imad and Ibrahim met, Imad recognized Huda and a painting of Fuad. When he was shown a photograph of Ibrahim and asked who it was, Imad said "me."

He identified not only which bed was Ibrahim's but the position it had been in just before Ibrahim's death so that, having tuberculosis, he could talk to his friends through the window.

Later, when Imad was 11, he recognized a man who had joined the army the same day as Ibrahim had.

At the age of two, he ran out in the street to embrace a man who had lived close to Ibrahim's family, saying, "you were my neighbor."

There were also several respects in which Imad's behavior corresponded to that of Ibrahim's: When he first learned to walk, he took great pleasure in it, saying, "Look, I can walk now" (Ibrahim's tuberculosis had made him bedfast the last 6 months of his life). When Imad was 2, he was already drinking bitter tea and coffee like a grown man. When he was 3 and a half and lying on the bed with his mother, he asked her to act as "Jamileh" would.

Imad had a passion for hunting and, after meeting Ibrahim's family, particularly wanted to hunt with Ibrahim's rifle, pointing out that he, after all, had bought it.

He was precocious in French (which Ibrahim had learned while in the army).

Imad had a phobia of large trucks and buses (Ibrahim's beloved cousin had been killed by a truck and Ibrahim himself had had a bus accident that injured some passengers).

Although Imad's family belonged to the Yasbaki political party, Imad himself was fiercely devoted to the Joumblati party (to which Ibrahim, who knew Joumblat personally, belonged).

Imad said that as Ibrahim he, planning to elope with Jamileh, had bought the license. However, forbidding the marriage because she belonged to the wrong political party, Ibrahim's family found and tore up the license.[17]

The William George Family

The evidence for reincarnation (however it be understood) goes beyond the memories, the recognitions, and the behavioral correspondences illustrated in the case of Imad/Ibrahim. In many cases, a child who claims to remember a previous life will also have birthmarks or congenital defects that correspond either to marks on the prior personality's body or to the cause of that person's death.

One example is provided by a case among Tlingit Indians of southeastern Alaska. (The Tlingit Indians evidently migrated from Siberia across what is now the Bering Strait some thousands of years ago.) A celebrated fisherman named William George had said to his favorite son, Reginald: "If there is anything to this rebirth business, I will come back and be your son. And you will recognize me because I will have birthmarks like the ones I now have," pointing to birth marks on his left shoulder and left forearm.

Later, William gave Reginald his gold watch, saying, "I'll come back. Keep this watch for me. I am going to be your son." Reginald then gave the watch to his wife, Susan George, who placed it in a jewel box.[18]

A few weeks later, William George disappeared from his fishing boat and his body was never found. Shortly thereafter, Susan George became pregnant and, during labor, had a dream in which her father-in-law appeared to her. (Such "announcing dreams" are not uncommon in Tlingit culture.) Susan gave birth barely nine months after the death of her father-in-law. Seeing birth marks of the same shape and location as those on the baby's grandfather, Reginald and Susan named their son William George Jr.

Taken in isolation, this case might be thought to involve nothing more than coincidence. However, Stevenson found the incidence of corresponding birthmarks and congenital defects quite high. There are claims for them, he said, in about 35 percent of all reported veridical cases, and the actual incidence of corresponding birthmarks and other defects may be considerably higher: In 49 cases for which the medical records of the prior person were obtained, clear correspondences occurred in 88 percent of the cases.[19]

Congenital defects in cases studied by Stevenson sometimes resulted from gunshot wounds. He had 18 cases in which the two birth defects, on subjects who recalled dying from a gunshot wound, corresponded to the places of the entrance and exit wounds. In 14 of these cases, furthermore, one mark was larger than the other, and in nine of these the smaller and larger wounds clearly corresponded, respectively, to the entry and exit wounds.[20]

Considering birthmarks and congenital defects highly evidential,

Stevenson devoted a lot of time to writing about them: In 1997, he published a 2-volume study entitled *Reincarnation and Biology: A Contribution to the Etiology of Birthmarks and Birth Defects*. Stevenson also published a briefer volume called *Where Reincarnation and Biology Intersect*.[21]

Back to the William Georges: There were also other features suggesting that William George Jr. was a reincarnation of his grandfather. For example:

He was the only one of Reginald and Susan's ten children to be born with birthmarks like those of his grandfather.

He had a gait similar to that of his grandfather, who as a teenager suffered an injury to his right ankle, which left him with a limp and his right foot pointing outwards.

He had a precocious knowledge of fishing and boats, but manifested a great fear of water.

One day, after Susan had opened her jewelry box to inspect it, the boy happened to see his grandfather's timepiece for the first time. In response, he said: "That's my watch."

The boy referred to his relatives by the names his grandfather would have used. For example, he spoke of Reginald's brothers and sisters as his sons and daughters; and he called his great-aunt "sister."[22]

A Hairy Birth Mark Case in Turkey

Seeing that a summary of this case provided by Geddes MacGregor in his *Reincarnation in Christianity* could not be improved, I have simply quoted it:

> One of [Stevenson's subjects], a Turk, claimed to have been, in his previous life, a gangster in Istanbul who was killed in a struggle with police. He pointed to a spot on his head where, he claimed, the bullet had entered. Stevenson, after having made a notation of the facts as claimed, reflected that if the bullet had entered the Turk's head at the spot and in the direction that had been indicated in the claim, then it must have exited at another spot, the location of which could be approximately determined. He then went back to re-examine the Turk's head. The hair was bushy at the [hypothesized] spot, so that no birthmark could be easily detected. After Stevenson had parted the Turk's hair, however, he found exactly the sort of second birthmark he had [hypothesized].[23]

[Although the text twice had "hypothecated" in this paragraph, MacGregor clearly meant "hypothesized."]

Those who do not know Stevenson's work may, naturally enough, be suspicious that these first three cases were simply too good to be true—that they must be fraudulent. Those who knew Stevenson and his work, however, realize that this possibility is too remote to be seriously entertained.

In any event, he also gave detailed reports of many other cases that he had investigated personally.[24] Following are a few examples (although in the case of Ma Tin Aung Myo, the previous personality was not located).

Samuel Helender

Samuel Helender was born in Helsinki in 1976. At a very young age, he started making statements and recognitions suggesting that he was identifying with his mother's younger brother, Perrti, who had died in 1975 of uncontrolled diabetes mellitus when he was 18 years old. Pertti's mother, Anneli Lagerqvist, who had remarried after divorcing Pertti's father, grieved deeply when Pertti died, as did his sister, Marja Helender (who would become Samuel's mother). When Marja was ten weeks pregnant with Samuel, she dreamed about Pertti. She had been considering an abortion, but in the dream she heard Pertti say, "Keep that child."

When Samuel was about a year and a half old, he was asked his name, and he replied "Pelti." (It would be several years before he could pronounce the "r" in "Pertti.") He could not be convinced that his name was "Samuel." He did not talk about his previous life except when photos or objects reminded him. For example, one photograph reminded him that a dog had bitten his leg. Whenever the family looked through the family album, and each time Samuel saw a photo of Pertti, he would say "That's me." Whenever he saw a photo of Pertti's father, he would identify it as "my father." Samuel did not speak directly about Pertti's death, but when he was taken to Pertti's grave, he said: "This is my grave."

In addition, Samuel would call his parents by their first names, Pentti and Marja, and told Marja, "You are not my mother." He continued calling Anneli Lagerqvist "Mother" until he was five.

On Christmas 1978, when Samuel was two and a half years old, he went around the room and kissed everyone present—just as Pertti had done.

Gopal Gupta

Gopal Gupta lived in Delhi, India, with his lower middle-class family. When Gopal was two and a half, his father told him to pick up a water glass that a guest had used. Gopal replied: "I won't pick it up. I am a Sharma" (Sharmas are members of the Brahmins, India's highest caste). Asked to explain his rude behavior, he said he had lived in Mathura, a city about 160 miles from Delhi; his name was Shaktipal Sharma and he had lived in a large house with many servants; he had owned a company called Such Shancharak; and he had had a wife and two brothers. During an argument, one of the brothers had shot and killed Shaktipal Sharma.[25]

Although his father at first did not have much interest in Gopal's story, he did mention the story to a friend, who had heard about the murder. The father then met the sales manager, who confirmed the story about the murder. Gopal was then invited to Mathura, where he recognized people and places known to Shaktipal Sharma.

Ma Tin Aung Myo

It is generally possible for the sex of the previous personality in a reincarnation case to differ from that of the child who remembers that personality.

There is great variation in the beliefs about, and the occurrence of, such cases. For example, Jains and Druses maintain that sex change is impossible. But in other cultures, sex-change is not forbidden. In the Athabascan tribe of Canada's Northwest Territories, approximately 50 percent of the children did not retain the sex of the previous personality. In the remaining cultures, the incidence of sex-change cases fall in between these two extremes, with the incidence being "3 percent in India, 9 percent in Sri Lanka, 13 percent in Thailand, 15 percent in the United States (nontribal cases), and 26 percent in Burma."[26]

Another interesting fact is that in all cultures in which sex-change is allowed (except for the Igbo of Nigeria), the number of reported sex-changes from female to male greatly outnumber the reported switches from male to female. These figures may accurately reflect the situation. But it is also possible that the number of male-to-female switches may be undercounted, because in many cultures it has been considered better to be born a man than to be born a woman, so a male-to-female switch from male to female might be viewed as a demotion.

Ma Tin Aung Myo provides an example of a sex-change case.

In 1953, a young Burmese woman named Daw Aye Tin gave birth to a baby daughter, whom she named Tin Aung. It turned out that this girl had some very distinctive traits. For example, she had a phobia of airplanes that was so severe that she was immobilized by terror whenever a plane flew over. Also, she disliked Americans and the British. When she was four and caught weeping, she explained that she was pining for Japan. In addition, she did not like Burma's food, which is spicy, but instead preferred sweet food and half-raw fish.

Moreover, her features and behavior were extremely boyish. Indeed, she changed her name from Tin Aung to Ma Tin Aung Myo to make the name more clearly masculine. (She would get annoyed if her sisters called her simply "Tin Aung.") She combed her hair like a boy and would only wear boy's clothes. For this reason, her formal education came to an end, as she was not allowed to attend school because she refused to wear "appropriate feminine attire." She also would only play boys' games, such as football and caneball. Finally, she said that when it came time for her to get married, she would want a wife.

Her airplane phobia, her boyishness, and her tastes became less mysterious to her parents when they came to believe that Ma Tin Aung Myo had been a (male) soldier in the Japanese Army during the occupation of Burma, and that this soldier had been killed when an Allied plane strafed the village. (The village contained Army headquarters, so it was sometimes targeted.) The villagers believed that the attacking plane was either American or British.

As for the birth of Ma Tin Aung Myo: Her mother, Daw Aye Tin, was a street food-seller, who became friendly with a Japanese army cook, doing business and exchanging recipes with him. When she became pregnant, Daw Aye Tin dreamed three times about the Japanese soldier, who said in a dream that he would come to stay with her and her husband. In any case, she had a baby daughter she named Tin Aung, who had the characteristics described above.[27]

Susan Eastland

Ian Stevenson discovered relatively few children in the United States reporting memories of previous lives. Stevenson also discovered relatively few female children reporting such memories. But here is a case in which the subject was both female and American, followed by a male case.[28]

Charlotte and Robert Eastland, living in Idaho, had a loveable six-year old daughter named Winnie, who was hit and killed in 1961 by an automobile. The death of Winnie devastated the family, especially Charlotte. Although Charlotte knew virtually nothing about reincarnation, she developed a deep longing that Winnie would somehow return to the family. Then about six months after Winnie's death, Sharon, Winnie's older sister, dreamed that Winnie was coming back to the family. Two years later, Charlotte became pregnant again, and she dreamed of having Winnie back. She named her baby Susan.

When Susan was about two years old, she starting making statements suggesting that she was Winnie returned. When asked her age, Susan would say "six" (Winnie's age when she died). Expressing great interest in photographs of Winnie, Susan announced that they were of herself.

A most interesting event involved a cookie jar with a cat on the lid. When Winnie was still alive, Charlotte would play a game with the children. When one of the sisters wanted a cookie, the cat was asked how many cookies she could have. If Charlotte felt that the girl should have only one, she would imitate the cat's voice, saying, "Meow, you may have one." After Winnie's death, Charlotte packed the cookie jar away.

After Susan had become about five, Charlotte pulled out the cookie jar and filled it up. When Susan asked for a cookie, Charlotte, not remembering that Susan had not been taught the game, asked, "What does the kitty say?" Susan startled her mother by replying, "Meow, you may have one."[29]

James Leininger

Here is another American case. This account is from a popular book, which could create skepticism, especially because it was not vouchsafed by Ian Stevenson (he had already died when the book was published). But Jim B. Tucker (Stevenson's successor at the University of Virginia, and author of *Life before Life,* for which Stevenson wrote the foreword) wrote a blurb for the book, calling the story "a spectacular example of the phenomenon of young children who seem to remember previous lives."[30]

Two-year old James Leininger, the son of Bruce and Andrea Leininger, suddenly started having nightmares, waking up his parents with screams. He was screaming "Airplane crash! Plane on fire! Little man can't get out!" This started happening 4 or 5 times a week.

One day his mother bought James a toy plane, telling James it even had a bomb. He corrected her, saying it was not a bomb, but "dwop tank" (he could not pronounce "drop"). When asked who the "little man" was, he answered "Me." When asked why his airplane crashed, he said "it got shot." When asked who shot your plane, he replied, impatiently, "the Japanese."

Part of the Leininger's extended family served as an informal "panel" to try to figure out what was going on. One of them suggested that James was reliving an episode from a past life.

Bruce Leininger, who was an evangelical Christian, exploded: "Bullshit!" A true Christian could not believe in reincarnation. "Not in my house. There will be no such thing as a past life. Never!"

After a further nightmare, Bruce asked James what kind of airplane the little man flew. "A Corsair." Bruce asked where the plane took off from. "A boat." Bruce was dumbfounded. He knew that a Corsair was a World War II plane and that it was launched from an aircraft carrier. But how did his 2-year-old son know that?

Bruce asked James the name of the boat. "Natoma." Certain that he had found a flaw in James's story, Bruce said that that sounded like a Japanese name. But then Bruce learned from Google that *Natoma Bay* had been an American aircraft carrier that fought in the Pacific.

In a conversation with James about his dreams, he was asked the little man's name. "James." He was told that James was *his* name. He replied: "The little man's name is James, too." What was the little man's last name? He could not remember. Andrea asked if he remembered anyone else's name. "Jack Larsen."

Bruce was no ignoramus. As an undergraduate at Farleigh-Dickenson, he had taken a double major in political science and Russian Studies, and did graduate study in international relations at Columbia under Zbigniew

Brzezinski. He would use the methodological approach he had learned to problem-solving to unravel the mystery of his son, beginning with *Natoma Bay*, the Corsair, and Jack Larsen.

At stake for Bruce, he felt, was the integrity of his Christian faith, as well as the whole history of rational thought that he had studied in college and graduate school. He had dismissed the possibility of reincarnation as no more than New Age mumbo jumbo.

By chance, Bruce was looking at a naval book about Iwo Jima one day, and when James saw a picture of it, he told his dad that it was there when his plane was shot down. Further research led Bruce to discover that *Natoma Bay* had been at Iwo Jima.

He then discovered that there was to be a *Natoma Bay* Association reunion in 2002. Bruce got himself invited. While he was there, he asked a veteran if there were any Corsairs on the *Natoma Bay*, and a man said "No. Not that I know of." Bruce thought: He'd made his case. There were no Corsairs. James had gotten it wrong. Bruce had effectively debunked the whole story, along with the wacky possibility of reincarnation.

But Bruce also found that there had been a Jack Larsen on board. He wondered how James could have dreamed up the name of a real member of the air group.

Jack Larsen was still alive, but Bruce also learned another name, James Huston, Jr., the only pilot killed during the battle of Iwo Jima. Andrea excitedly said that this fact—that James Huston was *Junior*—fit with another fact: When their son drew pictures of sea battles, he signed them James 3. So little James had been remembering the life of James 2!

Records showed that Huston was killed at Chica-Jima, a Japanese supply base roughly two hundred miles from Iwo Jima. And the Corsair problem, which had seemed to Bruce to be a fatal flaw in his son's story, was solved: Bruce was given a photograph that showed James Huston Jr. standing by a Corsair.

More evidence: James Huston Jr. had a sister named Anne. When five-year-old James met her, he called her "Annie," and only her dead brother had called her that. Young James also knew that she had an older sister named Ruth.

Bruce Leininger eventually came to the view that the story of his son's experience "is a gift to those who need some tangible proof that there is something beyond death.... It reaffirmed his religious convictions [and] revived (rather than challenged) his faith."[31]

Purgatory

In his study *Reincarnation in Christianity*, Geddes MacGregor's major suggestion to make progress on reincarnation involves the idea of purgatory. He agreed that the medieval doctrine of purgatory was horrible, but he believed that it could and should be reformed. He wrote:

> The particular form of purgatorial doctrine that was developed in the medieval Latin Church had singularly unfortunate consequences. Not only did it lead to notorious practical abuses...; it disastrously obscured the subtler and more interesting understandings of the doctrine.... Because of the crudity of the later medieval form of the doctrine and the grave abuses that attended it in practice, the heirs of the Reformation were often extremely hostile to it. Much worse, however, were its effects in diminishing serious reflection on the whole notion of an intermediate state.[32]

Purgatory is better understood not as punishment, suggested MacGregor, but as purification, with the practice of remembering the dead in prayer made central. Remembering the dead, he maintained, was a natural development within the Church. But it makes no sense apart from a doctrine of an intermediate state, for there could be no use praying for those whose afterlife could be in no way affected, "as would be the case for souls who were already in a final state."[33]

If we are to consider the notion of an intermediate state at all, the question arises: Where is it? MacGregor asked: "is there any reason why it should not be on earth?" In other words, "The intermediate state might well be conceived... in the concrete terms of reincarnationist teaching."[34]

Endnotes

1. Arthur Schopenhauer, *Parerga and Paralipomena: Short Philosophical Essays,* trans. E. F. J. Payne (Oxford: Clarendon, 1974), II: 368–69.
2. Some European Christians endorsed reincarnation until the Council

of Constantinople (553), where belief in it was discouraged, perhaps even banned. Ian Stevenson, *Children Who Remember Previous Lives: A Question of Reincarnation,* revised edition (Jefferson, NC: McFarland, 2001), 36.

3. Geddes MacGregor, *Reincarnation in Christianity: A New Vision of the Role of Rebirth in Christian Thought* (Wheaton, IL: Quest Books, 1990), 29.

4. MacGregor, *Reincarnation in Christianity*, 15.

5. MacGregor, *Reincarnation in Christianity*, 36.

6. Thomas Ryan, "25 percent of US Christians believe in reincarnation. What's wrong with this picture?" *America: The Jesuit Review,* 21 October, 2015.

7. Ian Stevenson, *Cases of the Reincarnation Type, III: Twelve Cases in Lebanon and Turkey* (University Press of Virginia, 1980), 7, 186; *Children Who Remember Previous Lives*, 4.

8. Stevenson, *Children Who Remember Previous Lives*, 274n8; D. R. Barker and S. Pasricha, "Reincarnation Cases in Fatehabad: A Systematic Survey in North India," *Journal of Asian and African Studies* 14 (1979): 231–40.

9. Jim Tucker, *Life Before Life: A Scientific Investigation of Children's Memories of Previous Lives* (New York: St. Martin's Press, 2005), 213.

10. Ted Christopher, "Science's Big Problem, Reincarnation's Big Potential, and Buddhists' Profound Embarrassment," Religions, Research Gate, 17 January 2021.

11. For example, Robert Almeder, *Death and Personal Survival: The Evidence for Life after Death* (Lanham, MD: Rowman & Littlefield, 1992), and Carl B. Becker, *Paranormal Experience and Survival of Death* (Albany, NY: SUNY Press, 1993).

12. Stevenson, *Cases of the Reincarnation Type*, III: 10, 344, 356, 358; Ian Stevenson and Godwin Samararatne, "Three New Cases of the Reincarnation Type in Sri Lanka with Written Records Made Before Verifications," *Journal of Scientific Exploration* 2/2 (1988), 217–38, at 235.

13. Jesse Bering, "Ian Stevenson's Case for the Afterlife: Are We 'Skeptics' Really Just Cynics?" Bering in Mind (Scientific American blog),

November 2, 2013.

14. Bering, "Ian Stevenson's Case for the Afterlife."
15. Stephen E. Braude, *Immortal Remains: The Evidence for Life after Death* (Lanham, MD: Rowman and Littlefield, 2003), 181.
16. Stevenson, "A Case Suggestive of Reincarnation in Lebanon," *Cases of the Reincarnation Type,* 270–320. This case was considered his best by Stevenson at least prior to his 2-volume 1997 book, *Reincarnation and Biology.*
17. For all of the details about Imad and Ibrahim, see Ian Stevenson, *Twenty Cases Suggestive of Reincarnation,* 2nd ed. (University Press of Virginia, 1974), 273–320.
18. Stevenson, *Twenty Cases*, 231–41.
19. Ian Stevenson, "Birthmarks and Birth Defects Corresponding to Wounds on Deceased Persons," *Journal of Scientific Exploration* 7/4 (Winter 1993), 403–16, at 405.
20. Stevenson, *Twenty Cases,*
21. Ian Stevenson, *Reincarnation and Biology: A Contribution to the Etiology of Birthmarks and Birth Defects,* 2 Vols. (Westport, CT: Praeger, 1997); *Where Reincarnation and Biology Intersect* (Praeger, 1997).
22. Stevenson, *Twenty Cases Suggestive of Reincarnation,* 232–34, 240.
23. Ian Stevenson, "Characteristics of Cases of the Reincarnation Type in Turkey and their Comparison with Cases in Two other Cultures," *International Journal of Comparative Sociology*, II/I (January 1, 1970). Quoted in MacGregor, *Reincarnation in Christianity,* 39–40.
24. Besides *Twenty Cases,* see also Stevenson, *Cases of the Reincarnation Type, I: Ten Cases in India* (1975); *Cases of the Reincarnation Type, II: Ten Cases in Sri Lanka* (1977); *Cases of the Reincarnation Type, III: Twelve Cases in Lebanon and Turkey* (1980); and *Cases of the Reincarnation Type, IV: Twelve Cases in Thailand and Burma* (1983), all published by the University Press of Virginia. Also, Stevenson's files contain 2600 additional seemingly authentic cases that were investigated by other researchers in which Stevenson had confidence. Several other researchers, furthermore, began publishing the results of their own investigations, revealing the same kinds of patterns.
25. Ian Stevenson, "The Case of Gopal Gupta," *Children Who Remember*

Previous Lives, 56–58.

26. Stevenson, *Children Who Remember Previous Lives,* 178.

27. Ian Stevenson, *Children Who Remember Previous Lives,* 60–62; Karen Wehrstein, 'Ma Tin Aung Myo,' *Psi Encyclopedia,* 2017.

28. Ian Stevenson, "The Case of Susan Eastland," *Children Who Remember Previous Lives,* 79–83.

29. Stevenson, "The Case of Susan Eastland," 81.

30. Jim B. Tucker, *Life before Life: Children's Memories of Previous Lives* (New York: St. Martin's Griffin: 2008); *Return to Life: Extraordinary Cases of Children Who Remember Previous Lives* (New York: St. Martin's Griffin, 2015).

31. Bruce and Andrea Leininger with Ken Gross, *Soul Survivor: The Reincarnation of a World War II Fighter Pilot* (New York: Grand Central Publishing, 2009).

32. MacGregor, *Reincarnation in Christianity,* 99.

33. MacGregor, *Reincarnation in Christianity,* 100.

34. MacGregor, *Reincarnation in Christianity,* 106–07.

CHAPTER TEN

Why Human Souls May Alone Survive Death

A NOTHER QUESTION remains to be faced by an affirmation of life after death: Why, asked Corliss Lamont, if human minds or souls can survive the death of their bodies, can they alone do so? There is, to be sure, from the perspective of panexperientialism, no absolute necessity to make this assumption. But virtually all the evidence for life after death, and all of the *strong* evidence, involves human-level minds. If it is the case that human minds alone survive death, why should this be? As Lamont pointed out, an evolutionary perspective means that there is no hard-and-fast line to be drawn between human and other minds. Positing life after death for human minds, he concluded, forces one to posit it for Neanderthals, chimpanzees, rats, and even flies.[1]

Degrees of Soul

This conclusion would indeed follow if the reason for attributing the power to survive bodily death to human beings were, as in some philosophies, the mere fact that human beings have souls, in the sense of self-determining experiences. This is, however, not the case in Whiteheadian panexperientialism. Whitehead's philosophy, as he himself said,[2] is neutral on the question of life after death: Unlike materialistic philosophies, on the one hand, it does not rule out life after death *a priori*. Unlike some other philosophies, on the other hand, it does not define souls as inherently immortal. The question, then, is whether there are reasons to believe that the human soul might have the distinctive capacity to survive apart from the kind of body that was originally needed to bring it into existence.

The assumption that a humanlike body was originally necessary to shape a humanlike soul is an implication of naturalism, including theistic naturalism. What it rules out is any doctrine according to which high-level finite souls either exist eternally (as in forms of gnosticism) or are created directly, apart from an evolutionary process. There is, by hypothesis, an order among the possibilities, so that more complex ones presuppose the instantiation of simpler ones.

Panexperientialism agrees, accordingly, with the modern assumption that humanlike minds presuppose humanlike bodies. The only question is whether, once the evolutionary process has given birth to the human mind, this mind can then exist apart from the conditions originally necessary for its emergence. Can the fruit survive apart from the root? And if we assume that it can, why should this be distinctively true of human souls (at least on our planet)?

The first step in an answer is the simple fact that evolutionary emergences do occur. Higher-level minds in general have all sorts of capacities not possessed by lower-level minds, and human minds in particular have various capacities absent, or present only incipiently, in the minds of other primates. There is nothing dualistic or anti-evolutionist, accordingly, in the suggestion that the capacity to survive apart from a biological body might be unique to human minds. It might simply be another of its distinctive emergent capacities, along with its capacity for symbolism, which, although not absolutely unique, evidently far surpasses that of any other animals.

In fact, it is rightly said to be central to human uniqueness. As Whitehead said: With the rise of the human facility with symbolic language, a difference of degree became in effect a difference of kind.[3] A reasonable supposition, furthermore, would be that this distinctive capacity for symbolism, on the one hand, and the capacity to survive bodily death, on the other, are simply two dimensions of one and the same emergent power.

If this is true, then the power to raise the poignant question, "When a person dies, will he or she live again?"(Job 14:14), would be the sign of the power to do just that. From this perspective, part of the difference in degree that became in effect a difference in kind would be the unique ability to live apart from the bodily organism.

The idea of the capacity to survive separation from the body as an evolutionary emergent was suggested by Whitehead himself. In a context in which the issue of such survival had been raised, he said:

> The personality of an animal organism may be more or less. It is not a mere question of having a soul or of not having a soul. The question is, How much, if any?[4]

John B. Cobb, Jr., developed this idea of degrees of soul in a discussion that, although not oriented to the issue of life after death, is relevant to it. In a book in which Cobb developed the idea that the rise of human existence was fueled by a great increase in surplus psychic energy, Cobb suggested that the "autonomous development of the psyche," which this surplus allowed, involves two elements.

> First, the aim at intensity or richness of experience on the part of individual moments of the soul's life leads the soul to actualize itself in ways that are immediately rewarding to it, independently of their consequences for the organism as a whole. Second, successive occasions build upon the achievements of their predecessors.[5]

Having "more soul," in other words, includes the fact that momentary occasions, rather than living primarily for the moment, are strongly tied together through time in a personally ordered society of memory and anticipation. Each occasion of experience, accordingly, builds heavily on its predecessors and strongly anticipates its successors, in comparison with animals having less soul, whose momentary experiences are based more on their responses to their bodily needs.

In a personally ordered society of memory and anticipation, by contrast, the novelty in one occasion may be prehended by a subsequent occasion, thereby becoming part of the defining essence of the enduring individual. Because growth is thus possible, the person is called "living." Although endurance regularly incorporating novelty is characteristic of all souls to some degree, in human beings this mode of relatedness to one's own past and future is so central that the difference in degree becomes, again, virtually a difference of kind.

Although all animals have soul, accordingly, human beings have enormously more soul—in terms of creative energy, in terms of the power to engage in symbolizing activities, and in terms of personal order through time, so that human beings' concern for their past and future experiences may be stronger than their concerns for their bodily welfare. Given this perspective on the human soul, it might well have the distinctive capacity to survive separation from the body, without supernatural support.

The Resurrection of the Soul

In a lecture entitled "The Resurrection of the Soul,"[6] Cobb pointed out that liberal theologians and philosophers of religion tend to take issue with the idea that belief in life after death is essential to religious faith. For example, one prominent theologian, influenced by Charles Hartshorne and by Rudolf Bultmann's program of "demythologizing" Christian faith, wrote: "Whether or not we somehow manage to survive death for a longer or shorter period of time, I regard as a question of no particular theological interest."[7]

Theologians often are not as forthright. They may, for example, praise the "biblical" image of the "resurrection of the body" in contrast with the "Greek" image of the "immortality of the soul," saying that the former, unlike the latter, avoids an untenable, prejudicial dualism between body and soul. The biblical image, theologians such as Reinhold Niebuhr have argued, points instead to the goodness of the body as God's creation, symbolizing the fact that our total life, including its physical aspect, is of eternal significance. Niebuhr said that Christianity's chief contribution to this issue is "its championing the cause of personality in its unequal struggle with the unappreciative forces of nature."[8] In thereby rejecting the image of "immortality" and limiting their discussion to the "symbolic value" or "existential meaning" of the image of resurrection, such theologians deny, if only implicitly, the literal truth of any notion of life after death.

In "The Resurrection of the Soul," Cobb, having pointed to this widespread tendency, added:

> Yet the question of what, if anything, happens after we die has not disappeared from the range of human concerns. It has simply moved out of professional theology into other hands. Our sophisticated equivocations on this topic have contributed to our general irrelevance to the religious interests of our contemporaries.[9]

By "professional theology" here, Cobb, of course, meant modern liberal theology, which serves the previously labeled "mainline" churches, which are now increasingly called "oldline," due to their diminishing numbers and cultural influence. The topic of life after death is central, by contrast, to the thought of theologians who serve conservative-to-fundamentalist churches, which have been increasing in numbers and visibility. Although a correlation does not necessarily point to a causal connection, in this case it probably does. It is unlikely that liberal churches will regain their vitality apart from the emergence of liberal theologies in which life after death is central (as in my systematic theology, *The Christian Gospel for Americans*).[10]

The traditional terms for life after death have been "immortality of the soul" and "resurrection of the body." John Cobb has suggested that "resurrection of the soul" is a better term—which recognizes an element of truth in both of these older terms.[11]

The language of "resurrection" suggests that life beyond death is always a divine gift, based on the ongoing creative, empowering, grace of God. The language of "immortality," by contrast, suggests that the power to survive apart from the body is now, thanks to earlier divine influence, inherent in the human soul.

Put otherwise, the evolutionary process, which brought the planet's life to the point where distinctively human life could emerge, depended at every step of the way on divine influence. On the other hand, the continued existence of the human soul in a new environment, apart from the physical body, would surely be the most radically new mode of existence ever brought about through the evolutionary process. This new mode of existence would depend upon fresh divine influences, calling the soul into new adventures.

In contrast with the supernaturalistic form of theism, however, naturalistic theism holds that the ability to live apart from a bodily organism could not simply be bestowed by God on any level of soul. If it were, the fact that chimpanzees, rats, and even flies do not have this ability would be a matter of divine whim.

Referring to resurrection of the soul, thereby employing the term traditionally associated with life after death in Christianity, reflects this point. That is, God is able to sustain the human soul apart from its bodily organism only because this soul now has the inherent power (thanks to earlier divine influence) to be thus sustained. Not using the traditional phrase "resurrection of the body," furthermore, reflects the idea that that kind of resurrection would be impossible.

Interestingly, a good case has been made by Gregory J. Riley, Professor of New Testament and Christian Origins at the Claremont School of Theology, for the twofold proposition that the earliest Christians spoke of the "resurrection of the soul," and that talk of the "resurrection of the body" did not emerge until the end of the first century. Riley derived the term "resurrection of soul" from Tertullian (b. AD 155), the first Christian author to produce an extensive corpus of literature in Latin.[12]

Endnotes

1. Corliss Lamont, *The Illusion of Immortality*, 4th ed. (New York: Frederick Ungar), 116–17.
2. Alfred North Whitehead, *Religion in the Making* ([1926] New York: Fordham University Press, 1996), 107; *Adventures of Ideas* ([1933] New York: Free Press, 1967), 208.
3. Alfred North Whitehead, *Modes of Thought* ([1938] New York: Free Press, 1968), 27, 41.
4. Whitehead, *Adventures of Ideas*, 208.
5. John B. Cobb, Jr., *The Structure of Christian Existence* (Louisville, KY: Westminster Press, 1967), 38.
6. John B. Cobb, Jr., "The Resurrection of the Soul," *Harvard Theological Review* 80/2 (1987): 213–27.
7. Schubert M. Ogden, "The Meaning of Christian Hope," *Union*

Seminary Quarterly Review 30 (Winter-Summer 1975), 161.
8. Richard Wightman Fox, *Reinhold Niebuhr: A Biography* (NY: Pantheon, 1985), 38.
9. Cobb, "The Resurrection of the Soul."
10. David Ray Griffin, *The Christian Gospel for Americans: A Systematic Theology* (Anoka, MN: Process Century Press, 2019).
11. Cobb, "The Resurrection of the Soul."
12. Gregory J. Riley, *Resurrection Reconsidered: Thomas and John in Controversy* (Minneapolis: Fortress, 1995). Tertullian's use of the phrase "resurrection of the soul" is quoted on p. 63 of Riley's book.

CHAPTER ELEVEN

Our Fine-Tuned Universe and Panentheism

Since the nineteenth and twentieth centuries, atheism has been largely taken for granted among cultural leaders in the West. Darwinism was arguably the major influence in this development. The major argument for the existence of God had been provided by William Paley's 1802 book, *Natural Theology*, which argued that the manifold examples of design in nature point to the existence of a divine designer. Darwin argued, however, that that teleological argument was out of date. He wrote:

> The old argument of design in nature, as given by Paley, which formerly seemed to me so conclusive, fails, now that the law of natural selection had been discovered. We can no longer argue that, for instance, the beautiful hinge of a bivalve shell must have been made by an intelligent being, like the hinge of a door by man.[1]

Recently, a new teleological argument has been developed involving the inorganic world, which existed long before the plants and animals studied by Darwin emerged. According to this view, the universe has been "fine-tuned" to enable the possibility of life.

The New Teleological Argument

An early version of this argument was given by Lawrence Joseph Henderson, who was professor of biochemistry at Harvard University (and who was, incidentally, instrumental in bringing Whitehead to Harvard[2]). In 1913, Henderson published *The Fitness of the Environment: An Inquiry into the Biological Significance of the Properties of Matter*, which argued that "the whole evolutionary process, both cosmic and organic, is one," and that the universe in its very essence is "biocentric."[3]

In Henderson's 1917 book, *The Order of Nature*, he spoke of the various properties needed for life, adding: "The chance that this unique ensemble of properties should occur by 'accident' is almost infinitely small."[4]

In the 1970s, this argument was taken up by physicists, who argued that the universe was "fine-tuned for life." The argument revolved importantly (although not solely) around the four forces of physics: gravity, the strong nuclear force, the weak nuclear force, and electromagnetism. The argument is that, if the values of these forces had been slightly different, there would not have been a universe supporting life. Physicist Paul Davies said: "Had [the] exceedingly delicate tuning of values been even slightly upset, the subsequent structure of the universe would have been totally different."[5] For example:

(1) Gravity is extremely weak—being 10,000 billion billion billion billion times weaker than the strong force, but if it had been a bit weaker, the stars would have been red dwarfs, not hot enough for life. But if gravity had been a bit stronger, the stars would have been blue giants, so hot that they could not have lasted the billions of years it takes life to develop.[6]

(2) The strong nuclear force (within the nucleus of an atom) binds protons and neutrons together. This strong force determines the amount of energy released when simple atoms undergo nuclear fusion. When hydrogen in a star turns into helium, the helium atom is slightly lighter than the two protons and two neutrons that went into making it. So, 0.007 of the hydrogen's mass is converted into energy. But if this figure were 0.006 instead 0.007, protons and neutrons would not bond together, so helium could

not be formed. The result would be an all-hydrogen universe. But if this figure were 0.008 instead, then protons would bond together without the aid of neutrons, so that no hydrogen would remain. "What is remarkable," said Great Britain's Astronomer Royal Martin Rees, "is that no carbon-based biosphere could exist if this number had been 0.006 or 0.008 rather than 0.007."[7]

(3) The Weak Force (also within the atom's nucleus) is responsible for converting neutrons into protons. The weakness of this force allowed the sun to "burn its hydrogen gently for billions of years," thereby allowing the universe to have time to bring about life.[8] If this force had been much weaker, there would have been no excess protons to make hydrogen, leading to all-helium stars, which would not provide the basis for the emergence of life.[9] But if this force had been much stronger, then "the Big Bang's nuclear burning would have proceeded past helium and all the way to iron," making fusion-powered stars impossible.[10]

(4) Electromagnetism is much stronger than gravity—about a trillion, trillion, trillion times stronger. If gravitational attraction were much stronger, stars would burn so hot that their life spans would be too short for life to develop. If gravity had been substantially weaker, galaxies, stars, and planets would not have formed. Had it been only slightly weaker (or electromagnetism slightly stronger), stars would be colder and not eventually explode in supernovae, thereby removing the universe's main source of many heavy elements.[11]

Agreement and Disagreement

The view that the forces are as if they had been fine-tuned is not controversial. Physicist Paul Davies wrote, "There is now broad agreement among physicists and cosmologists that the Universe is in several respects 'fine-tuned' for life."[12] This view is accepted by traditional theists, deists, pantheists, and atheists such as Stephen Hawking, who wrote:

> The laws of science, as we know them at present, contain many fundamental numbers, like the size of the electric charge of the electron and the ratio of the masses of the proton and the

electron.... The remarkable fact is that the values of these numbers seem to have been very finely adjusted to make possible the development of life.[13]

The fact that our universe appears to be fine-tuned for life, it is generally agreed, cannot be simply explained as a lucky accident—at least in the normal sense, as when a poker player gets a straight flush and then, with no cheating, in the very next game is dealt four aces. Rather, it is generally accepted that some explanation is needed. Competing explanations have been offered.

The Simplest Explanation

The simplest explanation is that the fine-tuning was the work of an intelligent cosmic agent. According to mathematician and philosopher of science John Lennox in *God's Undertaker*, "the more we get to know about our universe, the more the hypothesis that there is a Creator ... gains in credibility as the best explanation of why we are here." [14]

This interpretation of fine-tuning has converted scientists and philosophers who had long affirmed atheism. For example, famous astronomer Fred Hoyle, who had been so opposed to theism that he rejected the Big Bang—the name of which he had sarcastically coined—in favor of the steady-state view of the universe, because it seemed less suggestive of theism.

But his atheism was "shaken," said Hoyle, by a discovery he made about the carbon nucleus.[15] This nucleus, which involves six protons and six neutrons, is formed by combining three helium nuclei. However, explained Martin Rees,

> There is negligible chance of all three coming together simultaneously, and so the process happens via an intermediate stage where two helium nuclei combined into beryllium (four protons and four neutrons) before combining with another helium nucleus to form carbon.[16]

Unfortunately, however "the beryllium nucleus is unstable: it would decay so quickly that there seemed little chance of a third helium nucleus coming along and sticking to it before it decays." Fortunately, however, the carbon nucleus has a "resonance" with a very particular energy that "enhances the chance that beryllium will grab another helium nucleus in the brief interval before it decays."[17]

Hoyle had predicted this particular resonant energy, which is just higher than the combined energies of beryllium and helium. Some experimental physicists then demonstrated this prediction to be correct.[18]

"Some supercalculating intellect," the erstwhile atheist Hoyle declared in 1981, "must have designed the properties of the carbon atom," after which Hoyle added: "The numbers one calculates from the facts seem to me so overwhelming as to put this conclusion almost beyond question."[19] Hoyle, however, continued to reject theism, understood as the view that God, besides creating the world, intervenes in it supernaturally. Instead, Hoyle affirmed deism, according to which God created the world but then never intervened into it in a supernatural way.

Another convert was British philosopher Antony Flew, who was called "the world's most notorious atheist" on the basis of his writings in the 1950s. After learning about fine-tuning, Flew in 2007 declared "the divine Mind" to be "the only viable explanation [for] the origin of the laws of nature."[20] Flew made clear, however, that he did not accept traditional theism. Calling himself a deist, he described his deity as "the first initiating and sustaining cause of the universe."[21]

However, most physicists and cosmologists reject this idea, partly on the grounds that science cannot employ God (or any divine force) as an explanation, even in a deistic way. Instead, they appeal to the idea that our universe is really a multiverse.

Multiverse as Alternative to Divine Creation

Given the realization that our universe was able to support life only because of an enormous amount of fine-tuning, it would be surprising if (a) our universe had come about by chance, without a purposeful creator, and if (b) it were the only universe. The possibility that our universe came about by chance would be so improbable as to be virtually impossible. This degree of impossibility would virtually entail that our universe was purposively created.

But for most cosmologists and physicists, this idea contradicts their idea of what science is. They believe the only scientific view is that the universe came about by chance.

This line of thought led scientists opposed to the idea of a divine creator to promote the multiverse idea. Although there are many versions of the multiverse hypothesis, it is basically the idea that our universe is only one of a large number (perhaps an infinite number) of parallel universes, each of which has its own laws. This hypothesis has been used as a basis for thinking of our universe, in spite of its apparent fine-tuning, as an "accidental universe."[22] The idea is that, given every possible type of universe, one of them was bound by chance to be a universe that promotes life.

Scientists on both sides of the issue agree that the multiverse idea has been motivated by the desire to avoid a divine creator:

(1) Arno Penzias, who won the Nobel Prize as co-discoverer of the cosmic microwave background, said: "Some people are uncomfortable with the purposefully created world. To come up with things that contradict purpose, they tend to speculate about things they haven't seen."[23]

(2) "The many improbable occurrences that conspired to enable our existence," wrote Stephen Hawking, would seem to be a miracle created by a benevolent God, "if ours were the only solar system in the universe." However, if there are many parallel universes, each with different laws, then the "apparent miracle" disappears: "the multiverse concept can explain the fine-tuning of physical law without the need for a benevolent creator who made the universe for our benefit."[24]

(3) Likewise, said Martin Rees, "if one does not believe in providential design, but still thinks the fine-tuning needs some explanation," the multiverse hypothesis provides an option.[25]

(4) Cal Tech's Sean Carroll, saying that most scientists "would prefer a theory that was completely free of appeals to supernatural agents," wrote: "Given the number of potential universes, it wouldn't be surprising that one (or an infinite number) were compatible with the existence of intelligent life."[26]

The multiverse hypothesis has developed quite a following. In addition to Hawking, Rees, and Carroll, many other physicists have written positively about it.

But many other physicists have written negatively about the multiverse hypothesis, criticizing it on several grounds.

Critiques of the Multiverse Hypothesis

Violation of Occam's Razor: One of the most common objections to the multiverse idea is that it dramatically violates Occam's razor, according to which, all other things being equal, the simplest hypothesis should be chosen. For example, Paul Davies said that "the multiverse represents an inconceivably flagrant violation of Occam's razor—postulating an enormous ensemble of essentially unobservable universes, just to explain our own."[27] To postulate billions or trillions—perhaps an infinite number—of universes, rather than a single deity, does seem to violate Occam's principle.

Not Really Scientific: According to Australian Luke Barnes, the multiverse idea "will surely forever hold the title of the most extreme extrapolation in all of science, if indeed it can be counted as part of science."[28] Several physicists, moreover, have argued that it indeed cannot be regarded as a scientific hypothesis.

Princeton University's Paul Steinhardt, after having helped create the multiverse hypothesis, rejected it. "It's not even a scientific theory," said Steinhardt, because "it allows every conceivable possibility."[29]

In an article entitled "You Think There's a Multiverse? Get Real," Perimeter Institute's Lee Smolin said that "the multiverse theory has difficulty making any firm predictions and threatens to take us out of the realm of science."[30]

English physicist and theologian John Polkinghorne wrote: "Let us recognize these speculations for what they are. They are not physics, but in the strictest sense, metaphysics. There is no purely scientific reason to believe in an ensemble of universes."[31]

Similarly, according to South African applied-mathematician George Ellis, "the case for the multiverse is inconclusive. The basic reason is the extreme flexibility of the proposal: it is more a concept than well-defined theory." Ellis added: "Nothing is wrong with scientifically based philosophical speculation.... But we should name [the multiverse proposal] for what it is."[32]

Cosmology's Greatest Crisis: Philosopher Roberto Mangabeira Unger and physicist Lee Smolin wrote in 2015 that the discovery of the fine-tuning of the universe led to cosmology's "greatest crisis of its short history." This discovery was a crisis, they said, because there has been no acceptable explanation for the fine-tuning.[33] On the one hand, Unger and Smolin simply presupposed (evidently), like most other physicists and philosophers, that the idea of a divine creator is unacceptable. On the other hand, they said, the multiverse idea is both unscientific (because it is untestable) and absurd, being an "ontological fantasy."[34]

Science Stopper: Another objection to the multiverse theory is that it is unscientific in a different sense—that it could be used as an excuse to accept premature answers. Columbia University's Brian Greene has admitted that it could be a "science stopper," saying:

> If true, the idea of a multiverse would be... a rich and astounding upheaval, but one with potentially hazardous consequences. Beyond the inherent difficulty in assessing its validity, when should we allow the multiverse framework to be invoked in lieu of a more traditional scientific explanation? Had this idea surfaced a hundred years ago, might researchers have chalked up various mysteries to how things just happen to be in our corner of the multiverse and not pressed on to discover all the wondrous science of the last century?... When faced with seemingly inexplicable observations, researchers may invoke the framework of the multiverse prematurely—proclaiming some phenomenon or other to merely reflect conditions in our own bubble universe and thereby failing to discover the deeper understanding that awaits us.[35]

Well-known physicist Heinz Pagels (who died prematurely and had been married to religious historian Elaine Pagels) was even more negative, saying that those physicists and cosmologists who took this approach were "gratuitously abandoning the successful program of conventional physical science of understanding the quantitative properties of our universe on the basis of physical laws."[36]

Unnecessary: Another reason for rejecting the multiverse view is that it is not needed to solve the scientific problems for which it was created. To understand this objection, one needs to know that the multiverse idea arose out of the idea of cosmic "inflation," according to which the expansion of the universe began with a very brief inflationary phase, during which the size of the universe accelerated very rapidly, doubling and redoubling many times in a very small period of time.

The hypothesis of this inflation was regarded as necessary to overcome some problems with the original Big Bang theory, such as the so-called horizon problem. The "horizon problem," also called the "uniformity problem," is how the universe could be so uniform. Uniformity usually comes about by the exchange of information. For example, when a door is opened between a warm room and a cold room in a building, the rooms will begin equilibrating toward a common temperature. Analogously, different regions of the universe should, according to the original Big Bang cosmology, begin with different temperatures, because of the random nature of the initial conditions. But through mutual exchanges of information, these different regions would have equilibrated. However, because of the expansion of space, some of the regions would be so distant from each other that they would be beyond each other's "horizon"—meaning that they cannot share information, because it cannot be transmitted faster than the speed of light. Accordingly, there could be no equilibrating between these regions. In fact, however, evidence indicates that all regions of the universe have the same temperature. How can this be explained?

The dominant solution is inflationary cosmology, which says that, in the first split-second after the Big Bang, the universe expanded exponentially, faster than the speed of light, after which the expansion slowed down. Before the brief period of exponential inflation, the whole universe was in causal contact, so that it could equilibrate to a common temperature.

According to Steinhardt, these problems can all be avoided by replacing the idea of a single "Big Bang" with that of a "Big Bounce"[37]—that is, an infinite cyclical universe (which is a version of the same basic idea that had been accepted by Whitehead).

Does Not Eliminate Fine-Tuning: Still another problem with the multiverse theory is that, although it was motivated by the desire to eliminate fine-tuning and thereby a divine creator, it does not really do this.

According to Paul Davies, "the scientific multiple worlds hypothesis merely shifts the problem up a level from universe to multiverse." Explaining why, Davies said:

> The multiverse comes with a lot of baggage, such as an overarching space and time to host all those bangs, a universe-generating mechanism to trigger them, physical fields to populate the universes with material stuff, and a selection of forces to make things happen. Cosmologists embrace these features by envisaging sweeping 'meta-laws' that pervade the multiverse and spawn specific bylaws on a universe-by-universe basis. The meta-laws themselves remain unexplained—eternal, immutable transcendent entities that just happen to exist and must simply be accepted as given. In that respect the meta-laws have a similar status to an unexplained transcendent god.[38]

Paul Steinhardt agreed, saying:

> From the very beginning, even as I was writing my first paper on inflation in 1982, I was concerned that the inflationary picture only works if you finely tune the constants that control the inflationary period. . . . The whole point of inflation was to get rid of fine-tuning—to explain features of the original big bang model that must be fine-tuned to match observations. The fact that we had to introduce one fine-tuning to remove another was worrisome.[39]

Continuing, Steinhardt wrote:

> I did not take the multiverse problem seriously at first even though I had been involved in uncovering it. I thought someone would figure out a resolution once the problem was revealed. . . . Unfortunately, what has happened since is that all attempts to resolve the multiverse problem have failed.[40]

There are many good reasons for rejecting the multiverse hypothesis and, therefore, to accept the idea of a divine creator. And there is one more reason: the need to avoid ad hoc hypotheses.

Avoiding Ad Hoc Explanations: It is generally agreed that one way to be anti-scientific is to employ ad hoc explanations. An ad hoc explanation is one that exists for no other reason than saving a favored hypothesis. That is, it is ad hoc because it does not help explain any other data. The multiverse idea, developed to explain away the apparent fine-tuning of the universe in order to save the hypothesis that the universe has no divine creator, can be considered the ultimate ad hoc hypothesis.

It might seem, therefore, that the multiverse and the idea of a divine creator would be in the same boat, because both would be ad hoc hypotheses. However, the idea that the universe was fine-tuned by a non-omnipotent universal mind is not an ad hoc hypothesis. As explained in my 2016 book, *God Exists but Gawd Does Not* ("Gawd" is shorthand for an omnipotent, male deity), a cosmic agent is needed to explain a wide range of features of our world, including mathematics, morality, truth, religious experience, logic, and rationality. Accordingly, to explain fine-tuning by reference to a cosmic mind as understood by Whitehead is simply to add one more reason for affirming his view of a cosmic mind.

To be sure, even with this doctrine, many scientists and philosophers will, in spite of all the problems with the multiverse hypothesis, prefer it to a divine explanation of fine-tuning. This preference would follow from the widespread assumption that only the multiverse explanation could count as scientific. This assumption was reflected, for example, in the title of an article in *Discover* magazine, "Science's Alternative to an Intelligent Creator: the Multiverse Theory."[41] That article assumes that the multiverse hypothesis is scientific simply by virtue of not being theistic.

A scientific theory about anything can be called a satisfactory theory if it, besides being coherent, is also adequate to all of the relevant facts. With regard to a theory of the universe, all of the facts are relevant. If one philosopher concludes that there are various phenomena that are explainable only by positing a cosmic mind, while another philosopher concludes that these phenomena must be ignored, the second philosopher's theory should not be considered more scientific than the first one simply because it does not posit a cosmic mind.

Panentheism

The new worldview advocated in this book requires a new understanding of the divine reality. Whitehead and Hartshorne advocated a view of the universe known as "panentheism." The term means "all in God." Panentheism is thus distinguished from pantheism, on the one hand, and traditional theism, on the other.

How Panentheism Differs from Pantheism and Traditional Theism

On the one hand, by saying that the world is in God, thereby saying that God is more than the world, panentheism is distinguished from pantheism, which, by saying that "all is God," simply identifies God and the world—a view that implies that God is evil as well as good. On the other hand, by saying that the world is in God, panentheism is distinguished from all forms of traditional theism, according to which our world was created ex nihilo in such a way that the very existence of a realm of finite beings is wholly contingent upon a divine decision, and according to which God can create miracles. Panentheism, by contrast, holds that the existence of the world, with its metaphysical principles, is integral to the divine existence.

How Whitehead's Panentheism Differs from Deism

As we have seen, one-time atheists Fred Hoyle and Antony Flew, on the basis of fine-tuning, switched from atheism to deism, which does not allow for miracles. The same is true of Whitehead's view. But Whitehead's view also differs from deism. He says that God provides ideal aims, or initial aims (short for "initial subjective aims"), for events. This is not supernaturalist theism: Because God provides ideal aims for *all* events, these ideal aims involve no interruption into the normal God-world process. But the ideal aims for different occasions differ in content. This is "particular providence for particular occasions."[42]

This idea was doubtless influenced by William James. In the "Postscript" to his book *The Varieties of Religious Experience*, James opposed the "universalist supernaturalists," who "obey the Kantian direction enough to bar out ideal entities from interfering causally in the course of phenomenal events." He advocated instead the "piecemeal" approach, which admits

> providential leadings, and finds no intellectual difficulty in mixing the ideal and real worlds together by interpolating influences

from the ideal region among the forces that causally determine the real world's details.

In other words, James rejected the view "that the world of the ideal has no efficient causality, and never bursts into the world at particular points."[43]

Panentheism as a Version of Naturalistic Theism

An important implication of the description of panentheism is that it is a version of naturalistic theism. Besides the fact that the universe—in the sense of some multiplicity of finite actualities—exists as necessarily and therefore as naturally as God, the most fundamental causal principles of the universe exist naturally, being inherent in the nature of things, because they exist in the very nature of God, rather than having been created by an arbitrary divine decision. They cannot, therefore, be divinely interrupted, because such an interruption would be a violation of the very nature of God.

To affirm panentheism is to say that the universe is a compound individual, so that there can be interaction between God and the world, including its tiniest organisms.

As we have seen, it is widely agreed that our universe seems to be fine-tuned for life and, in addition, that the recognition of this fact is widely thought to have forced people to choose between a multiverse and a divine creator. Indeed, as we have seen, the main motivation for pursuing the multiverse idea has been the desire to avoid affirming a divine creator. But to take this desire as a reason is irrational.

This point is made by deity-averse philosopher Thomas Nagel, who said in his book, *The Last Word*:

> It isn't just that I don't believe in God and, naturally, hope that I'm right in my belief. It's that I hope there is no God! I don't want there to be a God; I don't want the universe to be like that.[44]

But later in the book he said, "It is just as irrational to be influenced in one's beliefs by the hope that God does not exist as by the hope that God does exist."[45] Accordingly, scientists and others should do their best to avoid being unduly influenced by their hopes and fears, looking as dispassionately as possible at which alternative has the best evidence.

As to why many science-based thinkers have wanted to explain away fine-tuning in order to remove its support for a divine creator, they have usually done so, like Nagel, on the assumption that such a creator would necessarily be a supernatural being, which could interrupt the normal cause-effect relations, as exemplified by the above-quoted statement by Sean Carroll.[46] Another example: In explaining why he rejected the idea of a divine creator, Stephen Hawking said: "Religion believes in miracles," which "are not supported by science."[47] However, a divine creator responsible for fine-tuning would not necessarily be a supernatural, omnipotent being, who could interrupt the metaphysical principles of existence.

It is true that most of the thinkers who believe the universe has literally been finely tuned argue that it points to the existence of an omnipotent deity.[48] But that does not mean that the fine-tuning hypothesis requires an omnipotent deity.

Alfred North Whitehead, who endorsed Lawrence Joseph Henderson's argument that our universe is biocentric and that this fact is not accidental, clearly did not accept the idea that the creation of a universe suited for life required a supernatural, omnipotent deity.

Although Whitehead only occasionally cited recent books in his writings, in his *Process and Reality* he called the books by Henderson "fundamental for any discussion of [the order of nature]."[49] Whitehead made abundantly clear in *Process and Reality* and other books that he rejected the notion of a supernatural, omnipotent deity. For example, Whitehead did not accept belief in "one supreme reality, omnipotently disposing a wholly derivative world," in favor of the view "that the divine element in the world is to be conceived as a persuasive agency and not as a coercive agency."[50] Whitehead must, accordingly, have considered Henderson's conclusion—that the universe is non-accidentally biocentric—consistent with Whitehead's non-omnipotent deity.

Affirming panentheism, accordingly, removes at least most of the objections to explaining the fine-tuning of the universe by reference to a cosmic mind. Panentheism rules out miracles and, more generally, any type of supernaturalism.

It is important to keep in mind the distinction between what are usually meant by the "laws of nature" and the "fundamental causal principles of the universe." The latter is a metaphysical issue. The fact that all actual

Eleven/Our Fine-Tuned Universe and Panentheism

entities are instances of creativity, and that they have fundamental causal principles, is intended to be metaphysical, true of every cosmic epoch. By contrast, what are normally called "the laws of nature" are cosmological, applying to our particular cosmic epoch. It fits with the idea of our particular universe, our cosmic epoch, that Whitehead said that "'God' is that actuality in the world, in virtue of which there is physical 'law.'"[51]

But there is an apparent problem: The basic physical laws of our cosmic epoch are very finely tuned, but Whitehead said that God is not omnipotent. How could a non-omnipotent deity—a deity whose power is persuasive, rather than coercive—have fine-tuned the universe? Here is a suggestion.

Like C. S. Peirce and William James, who regarded the laws of nature as habits,[52] Whitehead considered the so-called laws of nature as simply the most widespread, long-standing "habits of nature," its "communal customs."[53] The reason why the God of process theism cannot bring about effects unilaterally in our world is that the divine influence always faces enormous competition from the past world. This past world largely involves well-entrenched habits, which are involved in long-lasting enduring individuals such as protons, molecules, bacteria, and eukaryotic cells.

However, prior to the beginning of our particular cosmic epoch, the realm of finite actualities was (by hypothesis) in a state of chaos, in the sense that there were no enduring individuals, not even extremely simple ones, such as photons, electrons, and quarks. So, although our universe was not created out of absolutely nothing, in the sense of a complete absence of finite actualities, it was created out of a state of no-thing, in the sense of a state of affairs in which there were no "things" in the ordinary sense of the term, namely, enduring things. Instead, there was, by hypothesis, a multiplicity of finite actual occasions, which were extremely brief events—lasting less than a billionth or even a trillionth of a second[54]—happening at random. Because there were no enduring individuals, these fleeting events embodied no habits, no principles other than the purely metaphysical principles.

The present cosmic epoch began (by hypothesis) with the creation of extremely small enduring individuals—such as quarks, photons, neutrinos, and electrons—with each such individual being a serially ordered society of actual occasions (such as electronic occasions).

In such serially ordered societies, each occasion embodies not only the metaphysical principles but also the more-or-less complex contingent form embodied in its predecessors in that society. Each such enduring individual, in other words, embodies a habitual way of being, which through its long-standing repetition of a contingent form gives this form considerable power to implant itself in future events.

But prior to the emergence of any such habits, the divine creator (which was called by Plato the Demiurge or artisan), in seeking to implant a set of contingent principles in the universe, would have had no competition from any contingent principles. In that situation, divine persuasion could produce rather precise effects. To use the language of Genesis, the creator only had to think, "Let there be xyzabcdefghijkl," and it came into being.

From then on, however, the divine aims would always face competition from the power embodied in the habits reflecting these contingent principles, so that divine persuasion would never again, as long as this cosmic epoch exists, be able to guarantee precise results.

In this way, one can understand how the fine-tuning of our universe does not imply the existence of an omnipotent deity, whose goodness would be contradicted by the evils of the universe.

Conclusion

The modern worldview made it impossible to explain the mind-body relation, making it seem like we humans do not really belong in our world because, except for us and other higher animals, the rest of the universe was thought to be understandable in terms of materialistic, mechanistic terms. Also, modern cosmology has implied that we do not really belong to the cosmos, because the universe came about by chance. Panentheism, by contrast, implies that today's universe has been partly shaped by divine influence.

However, the elements of a new worldview discussed here change the situation radically. The mind-body relation, which had bedeviled philosophy and science since the seventeenth century, has been elegantly solved by seeing that the brain is not composed of insentient entities (which Whitehead called "vacuous actualities"). And the discovery that our universe is biocentric suggests that we humans, far from being cosmic accidents, are high exemplifications of what the universe is all about.

Furthermore, the discovery of the fine-tuning of the universe provides strong evidence for a divine creator, a conclusion that can be avoided only by affirming the unscientific view of a multiverse, which Unger and Smolin called an "ontological fantasy." Rethinking the universe in terms of panexperientialism and panentheism means that there are no valid objections in principle to the simplest explanation of fine-tuning.

Finally, a universe created for life is much more likely than an accidental universe (if one were even possible) to have an afterlife for humans.

Endnotes

1. Charles Darwin, *The Life and Letters of Charles Darwin,* ed. Francis Darwin, 2 volumes ([1887] New York: D. Appleton, 1896): 279.

2. Victor Lowe, *Alfred North Whitehead: The Man and His Work, Volume II*, ed. J. B. Schneewind (Baltimore: Johns Hopkins, 1990), 132.

3. Lawrence Joseph Henderson, *The Fitness of the Environment: An Inquiry into the Biological Significance of the Properties of Matter* (New York: Macmillan, 1913), 312

4. Lawrence Joseph Henderson, *The Order of Nature* (Harvard University Press, 1917), 191.

5. Paul C. W. Davies, *The Accidental Universe* (Cambridge University Press, 1982), 90.

6. See John D. Barrow and Frank J. Tipler, *The Anthropic Cosmological Principle* (Oxford Univerity Press, 1988), 336.

7. Martin Rees, *Just Six Numbers: The Deep Forces that Shape the Universe* (New York: Basic Books, 2000), 54–57.

8. John Leslie, *Universes* (London: Routledge, 1989), 34 (quoting Freeman Dyson, "Energy in the Universe," *Scientific American*, September 1971: 51–59).

9. Paul Davies, *Cosmic Jackpot: Why Our Universe is Just Right for Life* (Boston: Houghton Mifflin Co., 2007), 143.

10. Leslie, *Universes*, 34.

11. See Robin Collins, "The Teleological Argument: An Exploration of the Fine-Tuning of the Cosmos," in *The Blackwell Companion to Natural Theology*, ed. William Lane Craig and J. P. Moreland (Oxford: Wiley

Blackwell, 2009); Michael A. Corey, *The God Hypothesis: Discovering Design in Our 'Just Right' Goldilocks Universe* (Lanham, MD: Rowman & Littlefield, 2001), Rees, *Just Six Numbers;* and Simon Friederich, "Fine-Tuning," Stanford Encyclopedia of Philosophy.

12. Paul Davies, "How Bio-Friendly is the Universe?" *International Journal of Astrobiology,* 2 (2003). The idea that the universe is in any sense fine-tuned for life was rejected in a 2011 book by Victor J. Stenger, *The Fallacy of Fine-Tuning: Why the Universe is Not Designed for Us* (Buffalo, NY: Prometheus Books, 2011). But Luke A. Barnes, in his essay "The Fine-Tuning of the Universe for Intelligent Life" (DOI: 10.1071/AS12015), argued that Stenger's argument "is so deeply flawed that its results are meaningless." Although Stenger wrote a response called "Defending *The Fallacy of Fine-Tuning,*" Barnes provided an effective counter-response, "In Defence of the Fine-Tuning of the Universe for Intelligent Life," Letters to Nature (blog), 2 May 2012.

13. Stephen Hawking, *A Brief History of Time* (New York: Bantam Books, 1988), 125.

14. John C. Lennox, *God's Undertaker: Has Science Buried God?* (Oxford, UK: Lion Hudson, 2007), 68.

15. Robin Collins, "The Evidence for Fine-Tuning," in *God and Design: The Teleological Argument and Modern Science,* ed. Neil A. Manson (London: Routledge, 2003) 184.

16. Rees, *Just Six Numbers,* 50.

17. Rees, *Just Six Numbers,* 50.

18. D. N. F. Dunbar et al., "The 7.68 MeV State in C12," *Physical Review* 29/3 (1 November 1953).

19. Sir Fred Hoyle, "The Universe: Past and Present Reflections," *Engineering and Science,* November 1981.

20. Antony Flew with Roy Varghese, *There is a God: How The World's Most Notorious Atheist Changed His Mind* (New York: Harper Collins, 2007), 121.

21. William Grimes, "Antony Flew, Philosopher and Ex-Atheist, Dies at 87," *New York Times,* 17 April 2010.

22. See Davies, *The Accidental Universe.*

23. Denis Brian, *Genius Talk: Conversations with Nobel Scientists and Other*

Luminaries (New York: Plenum Press, 1995), 164.

24. Stephen Hawking and Leonard Mlodinow, *The Grand Design* (New York: Bantam, 2012), 153, 165. For an insightful critique of *The Grand Design*, see Wolfgang Smith, "Response to Stephen Hawking's Physics-as-Philosophy," *Sophia: The Journal of Traditional Studies* 16/2 (2011): 5–48.

25. Martin Rees, *Our Cosmic Habitat* (London: Phoenix, 2003), 164.

26. Sean Carroll, "Does the Universe Need God?" *The Blackwell Companion to Science and Christianity,* ed. James B. Stump and Alan G. Padgett (Hoboken, NJ: Wiley-Blackwell, 2012).

27. Davies, *The Cosmic Jackpot*, 179–85.

28. Barnes, "The Fine-Tuning of the Universe for Intelligent Life."

29. Maggie McKee, "Ingenious: Paul J. Steinhardt," *Nautilus* 25 September 2014.

30. Lee Smolin, "You Think There's a Multiverse? Get Real," *New Scientist*, 20 January 2015.

31. John Polkinghorne, *One World: The Interaction of Science and Theology* (London: SPCK, 1986), 80.

32. George Ellis, "Does the Multiverse Really Exist?" *Scientific American*, August 2011.

33. Roberto Mangabeira Unger and Lee Smolin, *The Singular Universe and the Reality of Time* (Cambridge University Press, 2015), 353-54, 360.

34. Unger and Smolin, *The Singular Universe and the Reality of Time*, 117–19, 160.

35. Brian Greene, "The Multiverse," in *What Is Your Dangerous Idea? Today's Leading Thinkers on the Unthinkable,* ed. John Brockman (Harper Perennial, 2007), 120–21.

36. Heinz Pagels, *Perfect Symmetry: The Search for the Beginning of Time* (NY: Simon & Schuster 1985), 359.

37 Paul J. Steinhardt, "The Cyclic Theory of the Universe," Department of Physics, Princeton University; John Horgan, "Physicist Paul Steinhardt Slams Inflation, Cosmic Theory He Helped Conceive," *Scientific American,* 1 December 2014.

38. Paul Davies, *The Goldilocks Enigma: Why Is the Universe Just Right*

for Life? (Boston: Houghton Mifflin, 2008), 204; Davies, "Stephen Hawking's Big Bang Gaps," *Guardian,* 4 September 2010.

39. Horgan, "Physicist Paul Steinhardt Slams Inflation."
40. Horgan, "Physicist Paul Steinhardt Slams Inflation."
41. "Science's Alternative to an Intelligent Creator: The Multiverse Theory," *Discover*, December 2008.
42. Alfred North Whitehead, *Process and Reality,* Corrected Edition, ed. David Ray Griffin and Donald W. Sherburne (Free Press, 1978), 351.
43. William James, *The Varieties of Religious Experience* (New York: Collier Books, 1961), 403.
44. Thomas Nagel, *The Last Word* (Oxford University Press, 1997), 130.
45. Nagel, *The Last Word,* 131.
46 Carroll, "Does the Universe Need God?"
47. Hawking and Mlodinow, *The Grand Design*, 34; Stephen Hawking, interviewed by Pablo Jáuregui, "No hay ningún dios. Soy ateo," *El Mundo*, 26 October 2014.
48. For example: Robin Collins, "The Teleological Argument"; Richard Swinburne, *The Existence of God* (Oxford University Press, 2004), 97, 189. See also Swinburne, "The Argument to God from Fine-Tuning Reassessed," in *God and Design,* ed. Neil A. Manson (New York: Routledge, 2003), 105–123; George F. R. Ellis, "The Theology of the Anthropic Principle," in *Quantum Cosmology and the Laws of Nature: Scientific Perspectives on Divine Action,* ed. Robert J. Russell et al. (Vatican Observatory Publications & The Center for Theology and the Natural Sciences, 1993), 363–99.
49. Whitehead, *Process and Reality,* 89n2.
50. Alfred North Whitehead, *Adventures of Ideas* (1933; Free Press, 1967), 166.
51. Whitehead, *Process and Reality*, 283.
52. William James, *The Principles of Psychology* ([1890] New York: Dover, 1950), Vol. 1: 104; Charles Peirce, "A Guess at a Riddle," in *Collected Papers of Charles Sanders Peirce*, ed. Charles Hartshorne and Paul Weiss (Harvard University Press, 1931–58), Vol. 1: 38–94; Peirce, "A Survey of Pragmaticisms," Vol. 5: 480.

53. Alfred North Whitehead, *Adventures of Ideas* (Free Press, 1967), 41; Whitehead, *Modes of Thought* (Free Press), 154.

54. Even in our particular cosmos, there evidently can be events that endure for only a millionth of a billionth of a second. See James Sadler et al., "Ultra-Short X-ray Pulses Could Shed New Light on the Fastest Events in Physics," University of Oxford, 16 November 2015.

CHAPTER TWELVE

Whitehead and James on the Question of Life after Death

Most people who have been shaped by modern culture—especially its ideas about body and mind—have been led to consider life after death highly improbable, even impossible (as illustrated by Corliss Lamont). Such people would change their minds, they may say, if they saw any good evidence. But one can find, they would likely say, no good evidence. Edward Gurney, one of the early psychical researchers (who was mentioned in Chapter 8), parodied the position of such critics with regard to a report of an occurrence of interest to psychical research thus:

> The fact is so improbable that extremely good evidence is needed to make us believe it; and *this* evidence is not good, for how can you trust people who believe such absurdities.[1]

For example: Canadian philosopher Kai Nielsen, speaking from a materialistic perspective, said that no amount of alleged empirical evidence for life after death could lead him actually to believe in life after death. If "we think that the concept of disembodied existence makes no sense," he said, "then we will interpret the data differently." That is, "we will say, and reasonably so, even if we do not have a good alternative explanation for it, that [disembodied existence] cannot be the correct description of what went on."[2]

For this and similar reasons, such people tend to ignore the kinds of evidence reported in Chapters 6–9. Or, if they know of this evidence but have no way to refute it, they may say: I cannot explain these phenomena, but I know that continuing to be conscious after dying physically is not the explanation.[3]

However, if people become convinced of a worldview that allows for life after death, the conclusions reached by Western culture about this issue over the past three centuries might be reversed, thereby allowing people to regain the hope that life is ultimately meaningful, even for people who have not had a chance in this world.

Whitehead on Life after Death

Whitehead did not explicitly affirm the reality of life after death. This fact might be used to infer that he thought life after death metaphysically impossible. In his most explicit treatment of this question, however, he said, in his 1926 book, *Religion in the Making*, that his philosophy is

> entirely neutral on the question of immortality, or on the existence of purely spiritual beings other than God. There is no reason why such a question should not be decided on more special evidence, religious or otherwise, provided that it is trustworthy.[4]

In saying that his position is "entirely neutral" on this question, Whitehead meant that his doctrine of the human soul did not, like those of Plato and Descartes, entail that the soul would necessarily survive the death of the body, and also did not, like materialistic philosophies, rule out this possibility. He clearly indicated that his philosophy did not make life after death metaphysically impossible.

It might be significant that this book was dedicated to "EW," which meant his wife, Evelyn Whitehead, and she was the one, said his biographer, Victor Lowe, "who had been hardest hit by [their son] Eric's death [in World War I], and most wanted to know what religion meant to her husband."[5]

In reply to the fact that his book on religion did not make life after death metaphysically impossible, it might be said that this book reflects

Twelve/Whitehead and James on the Subject of Life after Death 149

an early stage in Whitehead's metaphysical development, so that this was not his final position. However, in *Adventures of Ideas*, one of his last writings, he again left open the possibility, as he had in *Religion in the Making*, that the human soul might exist apart from the body. Having defined the human soul as "a personal living society of high-grade occasions," he added:

> How far this soul finds a support for its existence beyond the body is:—another question.... [I]n some important sense the existence of the soul may be freed from its complete dependence upon the bodily organization.[6]

Whitehead's view on this issue may have been influenced by one of his closest philosophical friends while he was at the University of Cambridge, J. M. E. McTaggart. Whitehead said "I was an intimate friend of McTaggart almost from the very first day he came to the University, and saw him for a few minutes almost daily."[7] In response to the common view that all the evidence shows the brain-dependent nature of the mind (as represented in this book by Corliss Lamont), McTaggart said that the facts support only the proposition, "*while a self has a body,* that body is essentially connected with the self's mental life."[8]

Whitehead may also have been influenced by his friend C. D. (Charlie Dunbar) Broad, four of whose 19 books were on psychical research and/or life after death (see Chapter 5).

Finally, in writing his great work, *Process and Reality*, based on his Gifford Lectures, Whitehead was attempting to find a way to express immortality. In a letter to Evelyn Whitehead's most intimate friend, Rosalind Greene, Whitehead wrote, shortly before he was to sail from Boston to Scotland to deliver his Gifford Lectures:

> I am working at my Giffords. The problem of problems which bothers me, is the real transitoriness of things—and yet!!—I am equally convinced that the great side of things is weaving something ageless and immortal: something in which personalities retain the wonder of their radiance—and the fluff sinks into its utter triviality. But I cannot express it at all.[9]

The suggestion that human consciousness might continue after bodily death would be a continuation, or a revival, of musings Whitehead had had as a Cambridge Apostle. One time when it was his turn to read a paper, he entitled it, "Is one life enough?" The question voted on was: "Do we desire immortality?" He answered "Yes" and added the comment, "I want a sort of something." And when there was a paper on "Nirvana," and the question voted on was: "Should we object to annihilation?" He answered "Yes."[10]

In a previous book, I opined that, whereas Hartshorne definitely did not believe in life after death, Whitehead *probably* did not either.[11] Now I would say that Whitehead probably *did*.

In saying that a positive answer to the question of life after death could be given only on the basis of "more special evidence, religious or otherwise," Whitehead probably, as suggested in Chapter 5, had in mind—besides reported events associated with religions—the evidence from psychical research.

However, he did not, at least in his writings, deal with the discussions of this issue by the Society for Psychical Research. But William James did.

James on Life after Death

Although Krister Dylan Knapp's book, *William James: Psychical Research and the Challenge of Modernity,* is excellent in most respects, it seems to play down James's personal involvement in the issues, saying that James "was not a believer or a seeker," as if his concerns were purely academic. But James's "White Crow" declaration (see Chapter 6) showed that he was a believer, at least in telepathy. Knapp also said that James did not want to "advance a religious cause nor to undermine one." But with his radical empiricism, James clearly wanted to give people evidence to endorse a religious, rather than a nihilistic, view of the universe. James also stated that he had an "urgent intellectual need," saying:

> The most urgent intellectual need which I feel at present is that science be built up again in a form in which [the phenomena of psychic research] may have a positive place.[12]

Knapp said that James had "no inclination toward the survival hypothesis or personal need for religious belief."[13] But the books by Knapp and Deborah Blum provide material showing that this statement is misleading.

Twelve/Whitehead and James on the Subject of Life after Death 151

For example, when James learned about his father's death, he told his wife that it made him feel, as he never had before, "the tremendousness of the idea of immortality. *If only he* [my father] *could be joined to mother.* One grows dizzy at the thought."[14] Also, James wondered

> whether there can be a popular religion raised on the ruins of the old Christianity.... Are the much despised "spiritualists" and the Society for Psychical Research to be the chosen instruments of a new era of faith?[15]

On learning about the project of the cross-correspondences (see Chapter 6), James was impressed. Referring to the proofs of some work by Mss. Piper and Verrall, he said that "they were excellent proofs of cross-correspondence, so far as I have read the stuff." James even told F. C. S. Schiller that Richard Hodgson might "still be energizing somewhere." On the basis of the cross-correspondences, James encouraged Mrs. Piper to give sittings along "evidential lines," as distinct from merely "advice sittings."[16]

Also, the numerous turn-of-the-century deaths of leading members of the SPR might, said Knapp, have led James to end his commitment to psychical research. But instead, it inspired him "to explore the possibility of their souls surviving." Moreover, "the supposed spirit-returns of Gurney, Sidgwick, Myers, and Hodgson motivated James to forge an original theory of immortality."[17] This theory involves the idea that the brain is permissive or transmissive, rather than productive, of consciousness—analogous to the way in which "the keys of an organ have only a transmissive function. They open successively the various pipes and let the wind in the air-chest escape in various ways"[18]—an idea that, as shown in Chapter 7, psychiatrist Bruce Greyson recently endorsed.[19]

James did not hold that his theory was entirely original; he pointed out that the transmission theory was defended by F. C. S. Schiller in his *Riddles of the Sphinx*.[20]

James said: "I believe myself that the 'unseen world' is now the next thing in order to investigate." Knapp commented, "James was invoking the perennial question of what happens to the soul upon bodily death. From that point onward, immortality occupied his attention."[21] James's most important writing on this issue, "Report on Mrs. Piper's Hodgson-Control" (1909), dealt with sittings "indicating the possibility that an identity purporting to be Hodgson was communicating from 'beyond the veil.'"[22] In this essay, James sought to answer this question:

> Are there any unmistakable indications in the messages in question that something we may call the "spirit" of Hodgson was probably really there?[23]

James admitted that the evidence was weak in places, but he said that the cases "produce a cumulative effect on the mind," so that conviction goes from being possible, to being plausible, to being "probable in a high degree."[24] James concluded that the evidence "makes pretty strongly for something that represents the living RH [Richard Hodgson] being active in the results."[25]

So, we can conclude that William James and Alfred North Whitehead both held that life after bodily death was possible, that James finally decided it was actual, and that Whitehead likely did too.

Endnotes

1. Edward Gurney, *Tertium Quid* (London: Kegan, Paul, Trench & Co., 1887), Vol. I: 227–73, at 264.
2. Kai Nielsen, "God and the Soul: A Response to Paul Badham," in *Death and Afterlife*, ed. Stephen Davis (London: Macmillan, 1989), 53–64, at 61.
3. This attitude was illustrated by Dr. Richard Blacher in the chapter on OBEs, who ridiculed the idea of "spirits wandering around the emergency room."
4. Alfred North Whitehead, *Religion in the Making* ([1926] Fordham University Press, 1996), 111. (The Fordham University Press book, edited by Judith A. Jones, contains the 1926 version, which was published by Macmillan, and hence has the original pagination.)
5. Victor Lowe, *Alfred North Whitehead: The Man and His Work, Volume II*, ed. J. B. Schneewind (Baltimore: Johns Hopkins, 1990), 189.
6. Alfred North Whitehead, *Adventures of Ideas* ([1933] New York: Free Press, 1967), 208.
7. Alfred North Whitehead, *Essays in Science and Philosophy* (New York:

Philosophical Library, 1947), 116. In the 1948 paperback version of this book, published by the Wisdom Library (a division of Philosophical Library), the McTaggart passage is on p. 124.

8. J. M. E. McTaggart, *Some Dogmas of Religion* (London: Edward Arnold, 1906), 105.
9. Lowe, *Alfred North Whitehead* II: 245.
10. Victor Lowe, *Alfred North Whitehead: The Man and His Work, Volume I*, ed. J. B. Schneewind (Baltimore: Johns Hopkins, 1990), 140.
11. David Ray Griffin, *Reenchantment without Supernaturalism: A Process Philosophy of Religion* (Cornell University Press, 2001), 2.
12. *William James on Psychical Research,* ed. Gardner Murphy and Robert O. Ballou (Clifton, NJ: Augustus M. Kelley, 1973), 42.
13. Krister Dylan Knapp, *William James: Psychical Research and the Challenge of Modernity* (University of North Carolina Press), 144.
14. Deborah Blum, *Ghost Hunters: William James and the Search for Scientific Proof of Life after Death* (NY: Penguin, 2006), 78.
15. Blum, *Ghost Hunters*, 82.
16. Knapp, *William James*, 255.
17. Knapp, *William James*, 248.
18. This theory is enunciated in James's Ingersoll lecture, *Human Immortality: Two Supposed Objections to the Doctrine* (bound together with *The Will to Believe* [New York: Dover, 2016]). The organ analogy is on pages 14–15.
19. Bruce Greyson, *After: A Doctor Explores What Near-Death Experiences Reveal about Life and Beyond* (New York: St. Martin's Essentials, 2021), 118.
20. Wiliam James, *Human Immortality: Two Supposed Objections to the Doctrine* (Boston: Houghton Miflin, 1898), 29.
21. Knapp, *William James*, 249
22. William James, "Report on Mrs. Piper's Hodgson-Control," *Essays in Psychical Research,* Introduction by Robert A. McDermott (Harvard University Press, 1986), 253–360.
23. Knapp, 259; citing James, *Essays in Psychical Research.*
24. Knapp, *William James,* 260.

25. Knapp, *William James,* 260.

Conclusion

GIVEN THE POSSIBILITY that global warming may result in human extinction in the not-too distant future, the only secure basis for hope in our time lies where it always has: in hope for a life beyond bodily death. Even if the idea that humanity will soon become extinct turns out to be untrue, that fate will come about sometime, and it remains true that we will all eventually die, so the only empirical ground for hope lies in evidence for a life after death. I suggest this answer with fear and trembling, knowing that most of my friends and other people whose opinions I respect will hate this answer.

One reason to hate this answer is the fact that it has historically been connected to the idea of divine omnipotence, the worst theological doctrine ever invented. I have argued in several books why that doctrine has been a disaster. (One of Charles Hartshorne's most appreciated books was entitled *Omnipotence and Other Theological Mistakes*.[1])

A second well-founded reason to hate this answer is that some deplorable doctrines have been associated with the idea of life after death, such as the idea that at death, people are assigned to either heaven or hell, with hell understood as a place of everlasting suffering.

A third reason to hate this answer is that people who accept it too often treat our world as relatively unimportant, compared with the world to come. ("This world is not my home. I'm just a-passing through.") On this basis, they may hold that it is not very important to try to promote justice for Palestinians and other mistreated peoples; to do what one can to promote peace and cooperation among religions; to take vaccines and to do whatever else one can do to deal with pandemics (for example, Tate Reeves, the Republican governor of Mississippi, said in 2021: "When you believe in eternal life—when you believe that living on this earth is but a blip on the screen, then you don't have to be so scared of things"[2]); to do what one can to prevent destructive climate change from getting worse.

But these consequences do not necessarily occur. If I may be permitted to use myself as an example: I have long believed in life after death. And yet I spent almost three years working on a book asking whether the world can survive the CO_2 crisis.[3] I would now say, we need the Green New Deal.

In any case, I believe the reasons to hate the idea of life after death, as weighty as they are, are outweighed by the reasons I gave in the Introduction for affirming life after death.

Life after Death: A Summary

The dominant view among science-based modern intellectuals is that the idea of life after death is not one to take seriously. That conclusion, however, is virtually implicit in the presuppositions of these intellectuals, such as Corliss Lamont. According to these modern intellectuals, there is no non-sensory perception; the world is basically mechanistic; and the world contains nothing but physical bodies and forces.

James and Whitehead both rejected this worldview in favor of the ontology of panpsychism, or panexperientialism, and the epistemology of what James called "radical empiricism," and what Whitehead referred to as the fundamental nature of "perception in the mode of causal efficacy." Their combined worldview is more adequate than the modern worldview to the full range of human experience—as argued by Edward Kelly, cited in Chapter 5—including the evidence employed by psychical research. Observed from this perspective, the evidence for life after death is very strong.

The work of good mediums, such as Mrs. Piper on good days, confirmed by William James, should leave no doubt about the reality of extrasensory perception, the reality of which is presupposed by most of the kinds of evidence for life after death.

Mrs. Piper and others also presented strong evidence for life after death. This evidence is not conclusive, because it can always be interpreted in alternative ways. But in each case, one must ask whether the alternative interpretation is really superior to a survivalist interpretation. In many cases, it is arguably not. Skeptics about life after death tend to hold that the possibility of a non-survivalist interpretation argues for the falsity of a survivalist interpretation. That conclusion presupposes the idea that genuine evidence for life after death is very unlikely. But this book has argued for a new view of the universe, according to which life after death would not be as surprising as previously thought.

In that framework, the cross-correspondences project was especially convincing, making it very difficult to provide a coherent interpretation of the data while excluding the prima facie evidence that after dying, some of the founders of the Society for Psychical Research, such as Frederic Myers, sent messages that Leonora Piper, Margaret Verrall, and other women picked up by using automatic writing.

Veridical near-death OBEs show that people can be aware of events in their environments when they could not possibly be receiving visual or auditory information through their ears and eyes. These experiences show that the mind can have experiences that do not seem to depend on the brain. They thereby provide evidence (albeit not proof) that the mind or soul can continue to experience after the death of the physical body.

A common objection to using apparitions to support belief in life after death is that, if the capacity to appear and perhaps even speak really existed, we should expect much more evidence of this capacity than we have. For example, most people who lose friends and loved ones apparently receive no sign. However, studies of out-of-body experiences suggest that, while the ability to see and hear in an out-of-body state can be as good if not better than normal, the ability to speak or otherwise bring about physical effects is extremely rare. This difficulty in producing effects is consistent with the fact that, although a few apparitions speak, most of them do not; in fact, some of them reportedly seem to be trying to speak but cannot. And most of them leave no physical effects.[4] It is quite possible, accordingly, that the reason most souls do not put in an appearance after separation from their bodies is that they are unable to do so.

Veridical collective and multiple apparitions are difficult to explain apart from the idea that the apparent plays a role in the apparition. In a collective apparition, two or more persons see the apparent simultaneously at the same place. What is puzzling, if one thinks of it as simply a projection, is how each percipient sees it according to his or her own position and distance. In a multiple apparition, two or more persons at different locations see the apparition within roughly the same time period. It seems unlikely that two or more people would hallucinate the same apparition at roughly the same time. And it would be very difficult to explain the apparition as a hallucination from one of the people, sent telepathically to the other.

There have been hundreds of well-studied cases of the reincarnation type that have been veridical, in the sense that researchers have located the person whose life was evidently remembered by the subject. In such cases, the remembered person evidently continues to experience in a new body. At least in some cases, the reincarnated person appears to have had some freedom in choosing the woman who will become his or her mother. If so, this is a very mysterious process. How could the choice influence the pregnancy? But empiricism requires that we accept facts even when we cannot know how they came about.

In addition, children claiming to remember a previous life often have birthmarks or congenital defects that correspond either to marks on the prior personality's body or to the cause of that personality's death. If the prior personality died violently, such as from drowning or an automobile accident, the child remembering the death may have a corresponding phobia of water or motor vehicles. These are extra-mysterious processes. How does a dream result in a pregnancy with particular inherited characteristics? But the fact that we have no idea how these things happen does not mean that we are intellectually justified in denying that they occur, given the fact that such processes have evidently occurred time and time again.

If the very idea of reincarnation is rejected, how does one explain why a child would seemingly "remember" events that he or she did not experience? This problem is even more difficult if the child has birthmarks or congenital defects corresponding to those of the person seemingly "remembered."

This book examines the question of whether there is any objective evidence that provides a basis for hope for an existence beyond bodily death. Many people may say, after they have studied reincarnation, that they cannot consider it a source of hope (such as Bruce Leininger when he began his attempt to understand the strange memories of his son, James). However, people can disagree. Irving Steiger Cooper wrote a book entitled *Reincarnation: The Hope of the World*.[5] And even Bruce Leininger, as shown in Chapter 9, came to the view that the evidence provided by his son, James, "is a gift to those who need some tangible proof that there is something beyond death."

With regard to the use of cases of the reincarnation type as evidence for life after death: Many westerners do not like the idea of reincarnation. This may be in part because they falsely assume that reincarnation is necessarily connected to a particular view of karma. But this assumption is not necessarily correct. Even if it were, that fact would not be sufficient to rule out life after death, because life after death may take many possible forms. Reincarnation may be simply one of the ways that life after death takes. Evidently, even in locations where well-supported claims for reincarnation are relatively frequent, at most only one child in 500 or a thousand reports good claims for remembering a previous life. Reincarnation may be simply one stage along the way in a continuing journey, as Geddes MacGregor suggested.

Chapters 3–12 present a new worldview into which life after death fits much more naturally than it does in the modern worldview, which had been presupposed by most people who have rejected the purported evidence for life after death out of hand. If the idea of life after death is true, it implies a great change in our view of ourselves and the entire universe compared with the common modern understanding. That is one of this book's major points. Convincing evidence for life after death would imply a huge change in our understanding of the universe, comparable to our changed understandings of the lowest forms of life, of the mind-body relation, of human perceptual capacities, of evolution, and of the fine-tuning of the universe. This changed understanding could perhaps be called postmodern.

It might be thought that, although the section on fine-tuning makes a good case for a divine creator, this fact is not really relevant to the evidence for life after death. But it is, for at least two reasons. First, the existence of a divine reality is almost universally considered a presupposition of life after death (although it is important that this divine reality not be conceived in terms of traditional theism).

Second, given the fact that the modern scientific worldview has, as it is sometimes said, "no place for gods,"[6] it is remarkable that science today virtually compels acceptance of a divine creator, as argued in Chapter 11. A universe known to have been the product of a divine creator is more likely to have the preconditions for life after death than a godless universe, if such were even possible.

It is sometimes thought that the idea of life after death entails the idea of "the resurrection of the body," understood as the physical body, which is a mythological idea, because it would presuppose a miraculous intervention. Chapter 10 suggests that people who think of life after death (including the post-crucifixion appearances of Jesus) in terms of "resurrection" could better speak of "the resurrection of the soul."

Some Christians, to be sure, are attached to the idea of the resurrection of the physical body, believing that it is important. But arguably what we really care about is our stream of experiences. People who have near-death out-of-body experiences are generally pretty indifferent to their physical bodies. They identify with their ongoing experiences, not their bodies.

In any case, understanding life after death as "resurrection of the soul" makes it more plausible than thinking of it as resurrection of the body.

Whitehead may have believed in life after death (I came to think that he probably did), and some Whitehead-based process theologians, including John Cobb, affirm it. In his 2014 book, *Theological Reminiscences,* Cobb said that Christians should not dismiss the reported resurrection experiences of the apostles "because of the dominance of a really incredible worldview," adding that he personally "look[s] forward to a new adventure."[7]

Charles Hartshorne and some other process philosophers and theologians have explicitly rejected this belief. On the basis of statements by Hartshorne and some of these other process thinkers, it is often said, by both advocates and critics, that process philosophy as such rules out belief in life after death.

The truth is, however, that process philosophy's position on the mind-body relation makes life after death possible. What is most important about Whitehead and Hartshorne in this regard is not whether they personally believed in life after death, but that they were two of only a handful of twentieth-century philosophers included in the prestigious "Library of Living Philosophers" whose ontologies allow for its possibility. It is the ontology allowing for the possibility of life after death, not the personal opinion of Whitehead or Hartshorne (or any other self-identified process thinker) that belongs to the core doctrines of process philosophy. (I discussed the idea of "core doctrines of process philosophy" in the introductory chapter of my *Reenchantment without Supernaturalism: A Process Philosophy of Religion*[8]).

The dominant view among science-based modern intellectuals is that the idea of life after death is not an idea to take seriously. That conclusion, however, is virtually implicit in the presuppositions of these intellectuals (such as Lamont). According to these intellectuals, there is no non-sensory perception; the world is basically mechanistic; and the world contains nothing but physical bodies and forces.

But when viewed from the perspective of good mediums, strong apparitional experiences, near-death out-of-body experiences, cases of the reincarnation type, James's radical empiricism and pluralistic panpsychism, Whitehead's panexperientialism and his perception in the mode of causal efficacy, and Whitehead's and Hartshorne's panentheism, the evidence for life after death is remarkably strong.

The title of this book is *James and Whitehead on Life after Death*. As I have said, I have concluded that James definitely came to believe in life after death and Whitehead probably did. If I am right, this is historically interesting. But what is really important is what we should believe today, and there have been roughly a century of studies and reflection since their times. We have knowledge that James and Whitehead could not have had.

Although they suspected that evolution of life on our planet did not involve any ontological jumps, we know now that, as Lynn Margulis said, "choice and sensitivity are already exquisitely developed in the microbial cells that became our ancestors."[9]

There have been decades of scientific studies of near-death OBEs, which show that, as psychiatrist Bruce Greyson put it, "the idea that our minds—our thoughts, feelings, hopes, fears—are produced solely by our brains is not a scientific fact. It is a philosophical theory proposed to explain scientific facts."[10]

There have been hundreds of scientific studies of reincarnation, which show that children from many countries and cultures, including American Christianity, have manifested memories from the lives of previous people; in some cases, the memories are accompanied by birthmarks and congenital defects.[11]

And although Whitehead knew about an early, biochemical version of evidence that the universe is biocentric, this conclusion is now supported by physics, which shows that the universe must be a divine creation, unless one can swallow what Roberto Mangabeira Unger and Lee Smolin call an unscientific, absurd, "ontological fantasy."[12]

It is not irrational to believe in life after death. It may, in fact, be most rational, given the amazing universe into which we were born.[13] In addition, it has long been observed that those convinced of life after death—from Jesus and the first Christians, to those who have fought for civil rights, to those who have had near-death experiences—do not suffer from a debilitating fear of death that would prevent them from taking risks in pursuit of truth and justice.

Endnotes

1. Charles Hartshorne, *Omnipotence and Other Theological Mistakes* (Albany, NY: SUNY Press, 1984).

2. Xander Landen, "Tate Reeves Says Mississippians 'Less Scared' of COVID because They 'Believe in Eternal Life,'" *Newsweek*, 28 August 2021.

3. David Ray Griffin, *Unprecedented: Can Civilization Survive the CO2 Crisis?* (Atlanta: Clarity Press, 2015).

4. George Tyrrell, *Apparitions* (New Hyde Park, NY: University Books, 1961), 63, 77–80; Carl B. Becker, *Paranormal Experience and Survival of Death* (Albany, NY: SUNY Press, 1993), 47.

5. Irving Steiger Cooper, *Reincarnation: The Hope of the World* (Wheaton, IL: The Theosophical Publishing House, 1920).

6. For example, Gilbert Harman, "Is There a Single True Morality?" in *Relativism: Interpretation and Confrontation,* ed. Michael Krausz (University of Notre Dame Press, 1989), 381.

7. John B. Cobb, Jr., *Theological Reminiscences* (Claremont: Process Century Press, 2014), 305.

8. David Ray Griffin, *Reenchantment without Supernaturalism: A Process Philosophy of Religion* (Cornell University Press, 2001), 5–7.

9. Lynn Margulis, "Gaia Is a Tough Bitch," in *The Third Culture: Beyond the Scientific Revolution,* ed. John Broackman (New York: Simon & Schuster, 1995), 139.

10. Bruce Greyson, *After: A Doctor Explores What Near-Death Experiences Reveal about Life and Beyond* (New York: Bantam Press, 2021), 209.

11. Ian Stevenson, *Reincarnation and Biology: A Contribution to the Etiology of Birthmarks and Birth Defects,* 2 Vols. (Westport, CT: Praeger, 1997); *Where Reincarnation and Biology Intersect* (Westport, CT: Praeger, 1997).

12. Roberto Mangabeira Unger and Lee Smolin, *The Singular Universe and the Reality of Time* (Cambridge University Press, 2015), 117–19, 160.

13. For some of the reasons why I call the universe amazing, and also why I reject divine omnipotence, see my book *God Exists, but Gawd Does Not.*

APPENDIX I

Jamesian-Whiteheadian Philosophy as Postmodern

IN THE 1980s and later, the term "postmodern" came to be applied to philosophies that emphasize skepticism, subjectivism, relativism, a distrust of reason, and a rejection of belief in objective truth. Today, that is the way the term is widely used.

But earlier, the term "postmodern" was used to describe Whiteheadian thought. Although the term was not used by Whitehead himself, the notion was implicit in his 1925 book, *Science and the Modern World*, in which he said that recent developments in both physics and philosophy have superseded some of the scientific and philosophical ideas that were foundational for the modern world.

Whitehead's most explicit statement about the end of the modern epoch occurred in a discussion of William James's 1904 essay "Does Consciousness Exist," the crux of which Whitehead took to be the denial that consciousness is a stuff that is essentially different from the stuff of which the physical world is composed. Whitehead suggested that just as Descartes, with his formulation of a dualism between matter and mind, could (with some exaggeration) be regarded as the thinker who inaugurated the modern period, James, with his challenge to Cartesian dualism, could (with similar exaggeration) be regarded as having inaugurated "a new stage in philosophy." Viewing this challenge together with that offered to "scientific materialism" by physics in the same period, Whitehead suggested that this "double challenge marks the end of a period which lasted for about two hundred and fifty years."[1]

Having described the scientific and philosophical thought of that period as distinctively modern, Whitehead thereby implied that his own philosophy, which sought to unite the philosophical implications of relativity and quantum physics with the Jamesian rejection of dualism, was distinctively postmodern.

Taking distinctively modern philosophy to refer to the "modern worldview" as characterized by a mechanistic and reductionistic view of nature that made harmony between science and religion impossible, John Herman Randall, Jr., spoke in 1944 of "post-modern" naturalistic philosophies, which overcomes the conflict with moral, aesthetic, and religious values, and referred to Whitehead as "one the pioneers" of this movement.[2]

The term was also applied to Whitehead's philosophy in a 1964 essay by John B. Cobb, Jr., entitled "From Crisis Theology to the Post-Modern World," which dealt with the emerging discussion of the "Death of God."[3] Arguing that the dominant modern mentality, which equates the real with the objects of sensory perception, excludes the possible causality and even reality of God, thereby leading to relativism and nihilism, Cobb portrayed Whitehead's philosophy as distinctively postmodern by virtue of the fact that his epistemology rejected the primacy of sense perception, that his ontology replaced material substances with events having intrinsic value and internal relations, and that he developed these ideas by reflecting on problems in modern science.

In his 1967 book, *God and the World*, and a 1968 essay, "The Possibility of Theism Today," Cobb restated his argument that Whitehead provided a postmodern vision in which theology is again possible.[4]

Cobb was not the only one in the 1960s and 70s who was thinking of Whitehead's philosophy as postmodern. In 1964, Floyd Matson, who was also influenced by Whitehead, advocated a "postmodern science," by which he meant one that overcame mechanistic, reductionistic, and behaviorist approaches.[5] In 1973, the term "post-modern science" was advocated at greater length and with more explication of Whitehead's position by Harold Schilling.[6]

In a 1976 book subtitled *Resources for the Post-Modern World*, Frederick Ferré, besides following Schilling in speaking of the need for the kind of "post-modern science" provided by Whitehead, also suggested that Christian process theology presents a "post-modern version of Christianity" that could help overcome the ecological crisis engendered by modernity.[7]

In 1973, Charles Altieri argued that it was Whitehead's philosophy, even more than Heidegger's, that best explains the connection between fact and value suggested by a number of American poets considered distinctively postmodern by Altieri.[8]

It is noteworthy that in a 1995 volume entitled *Early Postmodernism* in which Altieri's 1973 article was reprinted, the editor's introduction draws attention to the great difference between this early "postmodernism" and the type of thought with which the name later became associated.[9]

Endnotes

1. Alfred North Whitehead, *Science and the Modern World* ([1925] New York: Free Press 1967), 143.
2. John Herman Randall, Jr., "The Nature of Naturalism," in Yervant H. Krikorian, ed., *Naturalism and the Human Spirit* (Columbia University Press, 1944), 354–82.
3. John B. Cobb, Jr., "From Crisis Theology to the Post-Modern World," *Centennial Review* 8 (Spring 1964): 209–20.
4. *God and the World* (Philadelphia: Westminster Press, 1969), 135, 138; "The Possibility of Theism Today," in *The Idea of God: Philosophical Perspectives,* ed. Edward H. Madden, Robert Handy, and Marvin Farber (New York: Charles C. Thomas, 1968), 98–123.
5. Floyd W. Matson, *The Broken Image: Man, Science and Society* (1964; Garden City, NY: Doubleday, 1966), vi, 139, 228.
6. Harold K. Schilling, *The New Consciousness in Science and Religion* (Philadelphia: United Church Press, 1973), 44–47, 73–74, 244–53.
7. Frederick Ferré, *Shaping the Future: Resources for the Post-Modern World* (New York: Harper & Row, 1976), 100, 106–07.
8. Charles Altieri, "From Symbolist Thought to Immanence: The Ground of Postmodern American Poetics," *Boundary 2* (1973) 1: 605-42.

9. Paul A. Bové, ed., *Early Postmodernism: Foundational Essays* (Duke University, 1995).

APPENDIX II

Panexperientialism Compared with Dualism and Materialism

CHAPTERS 3 AND 4 introduced Whitehead's panexperientialism and how it solves the main element in the mind-body problem, which had been the central philosophical problem for modern philosophy since the seventeenth century. This appendix shows how Whiteheadian panexperientialism is superior to both materialism and dualism, which had long been widely considered the only two options. This discussion is relegated to an appendix, because it will be more difficult for most readers than the book chapters, and it is, strictly speaking, not essential.

The mind-body problem is: How can we explain the relation of our conscious experience to our bodies, especially our brains, so as to do justice simultaneously to two sets of beliefs: our science-based beliefs about the world, including ourselves, and our commonsense beliefs. UC Berkeley philosophy professor John Searle said, "the general form of the mind-body problem has been the problem of accommodating our commonsense and prescientific beliefs about the mind to our general scientific conception of reality."[1]

What are "commonsense beliefs?" There are two types, which I call hard-core and soft-core commonsense beliefs. Hard-core commonsense beliefs are ones that we all presuppose in practice, even if we deny them verbally. Denying them verbally would involve self-contradiction, because we would be implicitly affirming something that we were explicitly denying. Soft-core commonsense beliefs—what most people mean by "common sense—are not common to all peoples and can be denied without self-contradiction. When I speak of common sense, I am referring to hard-core commonsense beliefs. John Searle sometimes uses the term "common sense" to refer to the soft-core type.[2]

Three of our hard-core commonsense beliefs are our presuppositions (1) that we have conscious experience; (2) that this conscious experience, while influenced by our bodies, is not wholly determined thereby but involves an element of self-determining freedom; and (3) that this partially free experience exerts efficacy upon our bodily behavior, giving us a degree of responsibility for our bodily actions. Searle would not disagree.

The next two sections show that neither materialism nor dualism can do justice to these hard-core commonsense beliefs. The final section shows how the process philosophy of Alfred North Whitehead, thanks to his panexperientialism, can overcome the weaknesses of both dualism and materialism.

Materialism's Failures

Materialist philosophers have rightly concluded that dualism cannot explain how mind and body can interact because they are said to be different in kind, with the mind being wholly mental or spiritual and the body being wholly material or physical. But materialism fails even more fully, being unable to handle any of our three hard-core commonsense beliefs. This failure is especially serious, because these beliefs are presupposed in our moral life, which presupposes that we have a unified consciousness, with which we can respond to events and make decisions.

Insofar as it is accepted that science supports materialism, we have a serious conflict between science and our moral practices. This view also creates an apparent conflict between science and religion. For example, Francis Crick, in his book *The Astonishing Hypothesis: The Scientific Search for the Soul*, wrote:

> The Astonishing Hypothesis is that "YOU," your joys and your sorrows, your memories and your ambitions, your sense of personal identity and free will, are in fact no more than the behavior of a vast assembly of nerve cells and their associated molecules. As Lewis Carroll's Alice might have phrased it: 'You're nothing but a pack of neurons.' . . . The scientific belief is that our minds—the behavior of our brains—can be explained by the interactions of nerve cells (and other cells) and the molecules associated with them.[3]

This position, which stands in contrast with "the religious concept of a soul," said Crick, puts science "in head-on contradiction to the religious belief of billions of human beings alive today."[4]

However, the elimination of the three beliefs cannot be reduced to simply a problem between science, on the one hand, and religion and morality, on the other. That assumption would allow the typical modernist response: So much the worse for religion and morality! This facile solution is not possible, because this threefold belief, rather than belonging uniquely to a religious or even an ethical outlook on life, is part of our hard-core commonsense beliefs, which are presupposed in practice by human beings in all their activities—including their scientific activities.

This threefold belief cannot be eliminated from our repertoire of beliefs, as the position known as "eliminationism" proposes, because even if we deny this threefold belief verbally, we will inevitably continue to presuppose it in practice. For example, the recommendation by a philosopher that we eliminate this threefold belief presupposes that (1) we consciously understand the recommendation, (2) we can freely choose to accept the recommendation, and (3) our bodily actions, such as our "speech acts," can be guided by this free choice.

The denial of any of these three beliefs is, therefore, irrational: It involves a person in a "performative contradiction," which occurs, as UC Berkeley philosopher Martin Jay put it, "when whatever is being claimed is at odds with the presuppositions or implications of the act of claiming it."[5] Such performative contradictions, as Australian philosopher John Passmore pointed out, are self-refuting, because "to assert p is equivalent to asserting *both p and not-p*."[6] Avoiding such contradictions was central to Whitehead's philosophy, as he said that one must avoid "negations of what in practice is presupposed."[7]

Nevertheless, many philosophers affirm materialism. The present section of this appendix examines the thought of UC Berkeley philosopher John Searle, exploring why he affirms materialism and how he attempted to deal with its conflict with our commonsense beliefs.

John Searle's Materialism

In a book entitled *Minds, Brains, and Science*, Searle described the mind-body (or mind-brain) problem as

> the question of how we reconcile a certain traditional mentalistic conception that we have of ourselves with an apparently inconsistent conception of the universe as a purely physical system.[8]

The problem, more precisely, said Searle, is this: "We think of ourselves as *conscious, free, mindful, rational* agents in a world that science tells us consists entirely of mindless, meaningless, physical particles."[9]

Especially important for our purposes is Searle's claim that the problem is caused by what "science tells us." Searle's implied view is that the late modern worldview, with its materialistic reductionism, is not merely a philosophical interpretation that has been associated with science for contingent historical reasons. Rather, in spite of all the reflection upon the fact that theories are always "underdetermined" by the empirical evidence, Searle claimed that this late modern worldview is dictated by scientific evidence.

He argued, however, that two of our commonsense beliefs—that we have conscious experience and that this experience exerts causation on our bodies—can be reconciled with the scientific worldview. However, he fully admitted that his materialism cannot support the third of our three commonsense beliefs, freedom.

The Claim that Science Rules Out Freedom

In explaining why his materialistic position could not support the assumption that we have a degree of freedom, Searle stated:

> Our conception of ourselves as free agents is fundamental to our overall self-conception. Now, ideally, I would like to be able to keep both my commonsense conceptions and my scientific

beliefs.... When it comes to the question of freedom and determinism, I am ... unable to reconcile the two.[10]

In calling our conception of ourselves as free agents a "commonsense conception," Searle meant exactly what I mean by "hard-core commonsense beliefs." He said, for example, that no matter how many arguments against free will may be marshaled by philosophers, including himself, it is "impossible for us to abandon the belief in the freedom of the will."[11]

To be sure, he argued, it is possible to give up *some* commonsense convictions, such as the idea that Earth is flat. There is a reason why we can give up this idea:

> The hypothesis that replaces it both accounts for the experiences that led to that conviction in the first place as well as explaining a whole lot of other facts that the commonsense view is unable to account for.[12]

Searle here referred to what, in my terminology, is a *soft-core* commonsense belief.

But then Searle pointed to a different type of commonsense belief, saying that "we can't similarly give up the conviction of freedom because that conviction is built into every normal, conscious, intentional action."[13] Spelling out this point, Searle wrote:

> Reflect very carefully on the character of the experiences you have as you engage in normal, everyday ordinary human actions. You will sense the possibility of alternative courses of action built into these experiences. Raise your arm or walk across the room or take a drink of water, and you will see that at any point in the experience you have a sense of alternative courses of action open to you.[14]

Searle pointed out, thereby, that the kind of common sense involved in our belief in freedom is different in kind from the kind of common sense involved in the belief that Earth is flat:

> We don't navigate the earth on the assumption of a flat earth, even though the earh looks flat, but we do act on the assumption of

freedom. In fact we can't act otherwise than on the assumption of freedom, no matter how much we learn about how the world works as a determined physical system.[15]

To understand Searle's position, it is important to see that he is speaking of freedom in the real, or libertarian, sense of the word, not in the Pickwickian sense accepted by many philosophers, according to which freedom is compatible with physical determinism.[16] The distinction can be clarified in terms of Searle's statement, quoted above, that "you have a sense of alternative courses of action open to you." According to the compatibilist rendering of freedom, you may have a *sense* that you have alternative courses, but you do not, really: Although you may think that you made a genuine "decision," cutting off alternative possibilities, in fact the antecedent conditions dictated exactly the course of events that ensued.

For Searle, by contrast, the freedom that we all presuppose in practice rightly implies an affirmative answer to the question, "Could we have done otherwise, all other conditions remaining the same?"[17] This point is important, Searle emphasized, because "the belief that we could have done things differently from the way we did in fact do them . . . connects with beliefs about moral responsibility and our own nature as persons."[18]

However, although Searle's statement on freedom mirrors my view that belief in freedom is a hard-core commonsense belief, he did not take commonsense belief in this sense to be the ultimate criterion for a philosophical theory. He gave that role, instead, to the contemporary scientific conception of the world, which he simply called "science." He therefore concluded that our belief in freedom must be an illusion, in spite of its being ineradicable.[19] To see why he was led to this paradoxical conclusion, we must see what it is, in his view, that "science tells us" about the world.

Searle's position was indicated when he spoke of "the universe as a purely physical system" and "a world that science tells us consists entirely of mindless, meaningless, physical particles."[20] These statements reflected the standard modern conception, shared with dualists, according to which the ultimate units of the physical world are "purely physical" in the sense of being devoid of experience or sentience ("mindless"). Searle rejected the dualist's position, however, by insisting that the world consists *entirely* of

Appendix II   175

such particles. Indeed, Searle endorsed what he called "naive physicalism," defined as "the view that all that exists in the world are physical particles with their properties and relations."[21]

Pointedly rejecting the dualist's distinction between the brain and the mind, Searle said of the human head that "the brain is the only thing in there."[22] Indeed, Searle wrote of this as an item of "knowledge"—one of those things that, thanks to science, "we know for sure."[23] Far from being a property of a distinct mind, in his view, "consciousness is just an ordinary biological, that is, *physical,* feature of the brain."[24]

Given this conception of the world, it follows that, if one is to consider freedom to be real, one must be able to attribute it to the brain. That, however, is impossible: "Science," Searle wrote, "allows no place for freedom of the will." That assertion leads to the next question: "Why exactly is there no room for the freedom of the will on the contemporary scientific view?"[25]

It is, Searle answered, because all causation is exerted by physical particles:

> Since nature consists of particles and their relations with each other, and since everything can be accounted for in terms of those particles and their relations, there is simply no room for freedom of the will.[26]

Searle's argument, more exactly, is that science teaches that all explanation is in terms of bottom-up causation: "Our basic explanatory mechanisms in physics work from the bottom up."[27] The scientific worldview, Searle insisted, entails that this mode of explanation is to be used not only for the objects of physics in the narrow sense, but for *all* phenomena, and this point rules out freedom:

> As long as we accept the bottom-up conception of physical explanation, and it is a conception on which the past three hundred years of science are based, the psychological facts about ourselves, like any other higher level facts, are entirely causally explicable in terms of . . . elements at the fundamental micro-physical level. Our conception of physical reality simply does not allow for radical freedom [meaning freedom in the libertarian, noncompatibilist sense].[28]

Searle was factually in error in saying that this has been the conception "on which the past three hundred years of science are based." This totally reductionistic view came to be associated with science only in the latter half of the nineteenth century (except in France, where this transition occurred a century earlier). Prior to that, science was associated with the dualistic view, which emphatically did not accept a reductionist view of human beings, according to which their behavior was to be explained wholly in bottom-up terms. Searle's point would be largely correct, however, if it were modified to speak of British-American science since the latter part of the nineteenth century.

Searle was also presupposing an outmoded view of physics, according to which it reveals absolute determinism at the micro-level, whereas quantum physics now speaks of indeterminacy, which arguably betokens an element of spontaneity at the lowest level of nature.[29] Arguably, this indeterminacy at the quantum level becomes magnified in the human brain.

However, Searle ruled out this option, maintaining his insistence that human behavior is as deterministic as the behavior of billiard balls.[30] However, although there is no doubt that a human body, in the sense of a corpse, is analogous to a billiard ball, a living, conscious human being is not. Accordingly, to believe in freedom does not require supposing that the indeterminacies of the trillions of particles in the brain somehow magically combine on their own to produce our kind of freedom. Rather, the relevance of quantum indeterminacy is that, because the elementary particles comprising the brain are not rigidly determined, they can be influenced by the mind.

For Searle, by contrast, conscious experience is an "emergent property" of the brain in the same way that liquidity, solidity, and transparency are emergent properties of water, ice, and glass, respectively. In each case, the emergent properties "have to be explained in terms of the causal interactions among the elements."[31]

Accordingly, everything about the mind, including each of its seemingly free decisions, is said to be fully determined by the behavior of the molecules in the brain.

Having closed every possible opening for conceiving our felt freedom as genuine, Searle was thereby left with an irreconcilable contradiction between science (as he conceived it), on the one hand, and our ineradicable commonsense conviction of freedom, on the other hand. Faced with this choice, he assumed that "the contemporary scientific view" was more to be trusted, so that our feeling of freedom must be an illusion.[32]

Searle's conclusion reminds one of the criticism by philosopher Hilary Putnam, who taught at Harvard University, that most science-based schools of thought have produced "philosophies which leave no room for the rational activity of philosophy."[33]

The Efficacy of Mentality for Bodily Behavior

While admitting that he could not do justice to freedom, Searle claimed that he could do justice to the second of our hard-core commonsense ideas, which says that our minds' decisions are efficacious for our bodily behavior. The denial of that view is known as "epiphenomenalism," the doctrine that our minds are nonefficacious byproducts of our brains. Like most materialists, Searle wanted to avoid this conclusion because—as Jaegwon Kim of Brown University pointed out—it would be a reductio ad absurdum of the materialist position. But after studying this doctrine for many years, Kim concluded that materialism could not really avoid epiphenomenalism.[34]

The Emergence of Consciousness

Although materialism cannot do justice to freedom and the efficacy of consciousness, most materialists have believed that it must at least do justice to the most obvious of our three commonsense beliefs, the fact that conscious experience itself exists. As Searle said, if your theory results in the view that consciousness does not exist, "you have simply produced a reductio ad absurdum of the theory."[35]

But it is impossible for materialists to avoid this reductio, because of the assumption—widely assumed to be vouchsafed by science—that neurons are devoid of all sentience or experience whatsoever. There is simply no way to explain how sentient entities could result from insentient ones. New York University's Thomas Nagel, using the French term *pour soi* (for itself), for something that has experience, and *en soi* (it self), for something that has no experience, declared: "One cannot derive a *pour soi* from an *en soi*.... This gap is logically unbridgeable."[36]

Dualism's Difficulties

Advocates of René Descartes's dualism argue that it does not have as many problems as materialism, and they are right. The main strength of Cartesian dualism, in comparison with materialism, is that, by speaking of the mind as numerically distinct from the brain, it provides a basis for explaining two major features of our conscious experience: its unity and its freedom.

The Unity of Consciousness

With regard to the unity of consciousness, some materialists candidly admit this to be a problem for their identification of the mind with the brain. Thomas Nagel, for example, said that "the unity of consciousness, even if it is not complete, poses a problem for the theory that mental states are states of something as complex as a brain."[37]

Some eliminative materialists have tried to avoid this problem by saying that the unity of experience is an illusion. Daniel Dennett, for example, said that the head contains billions of "miniagents and microagents (with no single Boss)" and "that's all that's going on."[38] But if that were really all that is going on, even the appearance of unity would be a mystery.

John Searle was more candid: He included "unity" as one of the "structures of consciousness"—which he illustrated by pointing out that one can have experiences of a rose, a couch, and a toothache "all as experiences that are part of one and the same conscious event." However, he admitted: "We have little understanding of how the brain achieves this unity."[39]

Dualists avoid this problem by saying that the mind is a full-fledged actuality, numerically distinct from the brain. Neurophysiologist John Eccles, for example, said that "the unity of conscious experience is provided by the self-conscious mind, not by the neural machinery."[40]

Freedom

With regard to freedom, which we all presuppose in practice: the dualist position is again superior to materialism. Materialists find it difficult to affirm freedom because, if there are simply billions of microagents, but no overall "Boss," we could not make self-determining responses to the influences upon us. Dualism, by contrast, says that, besides the billions of microagents constituting the brain, there is another agent, distinct from the brain, which we call the mind, psyche, or soul. Being an individual, it provides a locus for the freedom we all presuppose.

Efficacy

This freedom, furthermore, is usually not limited to the power to determine our own mental states. Dualists generally also attribute to the mind the power to influence its body.

Those dualists who do not attribute this power to the mind, as has been discussed, affirm epiphenomenalism. Although the idea that the mind is simply a nonefficacious byproduct of the brain, with no power to influence the brain in return, was at one time quite prevalent, today most dualists reject it, agreeing with those who have argued that the efficacy of conscious experience for bodily behavior is too obvious to deny. Accordingly, "dualism" is usually equated with "interactionism," according to which mind and body act on each other.

At this point, however, dualists encounter difficulties: Although they may affirm interactionism, they have to admit that they cannot explain how mind and body can influence each other. They hence can be called "agnostic dualists."

One example is provided by Karl Popper, one of the twentieth century's most influential philosophers of science. At one time, Popper assumed that an explanation would be forthcoming, saying in an early monograph:

> What we want is to understand how such nonphysical things as purposes, deliberations, plans, decisions, theories, tensions, and values play a part in bringing about physical changes in the physical world.[41]

But in a later book, *The Self and Its Brain: An Argument for Interactionism*, Popper and his co-author, John C. Eccles, in effect admitted failure by trying to minimize the importance of the once-urgent problem: "Complete understanding, like complete knowledge," they said, "is unlikely to be achieved."[42]

Insofar as Popper did try to explain how the mind's efficacy upon its body is imaginable, he said: "I think that the self in a sense plays on the brain, as a pianist plays a piano."[43] Popper, however, had affirmed the self to be different in kind from the matter comprising the body, even accepting the pejorative description of dualism as belief in "a ghost in the machine."[44] He surely realized that a physical-physical (finger-piano key) relation can provide no help whatsoever in understanding the possibility of a mental-physical relation.

Geoffrey Madell

For another example of agnostic dualism, we can examine the position of Edinburgh's Geoffrey Madell. Assuming that dualism and materialism constitute the only two real options, he began his major work, *Mind and Materialism*, by saying: "Sympathy with the underlying motivation behind materialism must rest in part on an appreciation of the difficulties which any dualist position confronts."[45]

Then, in speaking more concretely of these difficulties, he said that "it is admitted on all sides that the nature of the causal connection between the mental and the physical, as the Cartesian conceives of it, is utterly mysterious."[46]

Madell included the first emergence of mind as part of this mystery, saying:

> The appearance of consciousness in the course of evolution must appear for the dualist to be an utterly inexplicable emergence of something entirely new, an emergence which must appear quite bizarre.[47]

Also Madell said the same for the emergence of sentience in each human:

> A parallel emergence occurs, the dualist claims, in the course of the development of the embryo, but it is an event of equal inexplicability.[48]

Madell rightly referred to his book as "a limited and qualified defence of dualism."[49] Seeing the difficulties he acknowledged, however, one might well wonder why he defended it at all.

The answer, which most of his book was devoted to supporting, is that whatever the problems of dualism, those of materialism are far worse. Materialism, he said, involves a doctrine that is "totally mysterious where it is not simply incredible." On that basis, he concluded that "interactionist dualism looks to be by far the only plausible framework in which the facts of our experience can be fitted."[50]

His argument for dualism, in other words, was primarily negative: Materialism is false, therefore dualism must be true. After his statement that he was offering only "a limited and qualified defence of dualism," he said: "The very factors which, to my mind, make materialism impossible to accept, point strongly towards some sort of dualist position."[51] The assumption, again, is that only these two positions are live options.

Madell did briefly mention a third position, panpsychism, but he dismissed it in one sentence, saying that it does not have "any explanation to offer as to why or how mental properties cohere with physical"[52]—a charge that at best applies only to certain versions of panpsychism, especially because he assumed that those who hold it affirm that the dualistic meanings of "physical" and "mental" remain unchanged.

Madell showed no signs of having examined the writings of any actual advocates of panpsychism or panexperientialism, referring instead, like most other contemporary philosophers, only to the Spinozistic version, according to which all things, including all aggregational things such as rocks, have a mental aspect as well as a physical aspect. One would think that, given the manifold difficulties that Madell pointed out in both dualism and materialism, this third alternative would have been examined more seriously.

Had he done so, he might have learned that Alfred North Whitehead—who gave his Gifford Lectures at Madell's workplace, the University of Edinburgh—provided a version of panpsychism or panexperientialism that has "some sort of dualist position." That is, if by "dualism" one is referring simply to the numerical distinction (not an ontological difference) between mind and brain, Whitehead's panexperientialism is dualistic in the sense of involving interaction between mind and brain.

And as we saw in the previous section, contemporary materialists are increasingly admitting that their own position also contains insoluble problems. They continue to affirm it, however, because they believe dualism, which they see as having even greater problems, is the only alternative.

Panexperientialism: The Neglected Alternative

One-time Oxford philosopher Colin McGinn thought he knew that materialism is true on the ground that all the alternatives to materialism are false. With regard to panpsychism, McGinn could not deal with it seriously. He simply said that he would "here be assuming that panpsychism, like all other extant constructive solutions, is inadequate as an answer to the mind-body problem."[53]

McGinn based this judgment on an obviously false version of panpsychism, which Whitehead, Hartshorne, and many other advocates do not affirm. According to McGinn's version, as explained in a previous book, "bits of rocks and elementary particles enjoy an inner conscious life" and "rocks actually have thoughts." With that understanding of panpsychism in mind, McGinn concluded that it is "metaphysically and scientifically outrageous" and "utter balderdash."[54]

McGinn's treatment of panpsychism was as bad as that of Karl Popper, who called it "fantastic" on the grounds that it attributes feelings to telephones.[55] But panpsychism as Popper and McGinn characterized it has virtually nothing in common with Whitehead's.

One difference is that Whiteheadian panexperientialism distinguishes between experience as such, which is attributed to even the lowest-level individuals (such as electrons), and *conscious* experience, which occurs only in higher-level individuals who could have emerged only after billions of years of evolution. Whitehead's philosophy does not affirm the idea that "elementary particles enjoy an inner conscious life."

McGinn and Popper were both guilty of the species-genus fallacy, assuming that a problem that applies to a particular species of panpsychism (such as Spinoza's) applies to every form of panpsychism. This fallacy also characterizes the criticism of panpsychism in Christof Koch's book *The Feeling of Life Itself: Why Consciousness is Widespread but Can't Be Computed*.[56]

Panexperientialism and Temporality

Panexperientialism is based upon the supposition that we can and should think about the units comprising the physical world by analogy with our own experience, which we know from within. The supposition, in other words, is that the apparent difference in kind between our experience, or our "mind," and the entities comprising our bodies is an illusion, resulting from the fact that we know them in two different ways. We know our minds from within, by identity and memory, whereas in sensory perception of our bodies, as in looking in a mirror, we know them from without. Once we realize this, there is no reason to assume them really to be different in kind.

This solution to the mind-body problem, interestingly enough, was suggested by Immanuel Kant in his First Critique (in which he supposedly quit asking what things are like in themselves). In a discussion of "the communion of soul and body," Kant said:

> The difficulty peculiar to the problem consists ... in the assumed heterogeneity of the object of inner sense (the soul) and the objects of the outer senses, the formal condition of their intuition being, in the case of the former, time only, and in the case of the latter, also space. But if we consider that the two kinds of objects thus differ from each other, not inwardly but only in so far as one appears outwardly to another, and that what, as thing in itself, underlies the appearances of matter, perhaps after all may not be so heterogeneous in character, this difficulty vanishes.[57]

A crucial event in the history of this solution to the mind-body problem, as University of North Texas philosopher Pete Gunter emphasized,[58] occurred between the first and second books published by Henri Bergson. In his first book, *Time and Free Will* (1889), Bergson articulated an absolute dualism between physical nature, which was described as spatial but nontemporal, and the mind, which was described in terms of temporal duration. Bergson soon realized, however, that this made the interaction of mind and matter, which he presupposed, unintelligible.[59]

In his next book, *Matter and Memory* (1896), Bergson overcame this dualism by attributing a primitive memory and thereby temporal duration to that which we, from without, call matter. The ultimate units of the universe, in other words, are not purely spatial bits of matter but spatial-temporal events, with temporal as well as spatial extension. With the dualism overcome, mind-body interaction could be understood as a purely natural occurrence.

This Bergsonian solution was developed more fully by Whitehead. The fundamental units of the actual world, the fully actual entities, were said by Whitehead to be "actual occasions," by which he meant that they were temporally as well as spatially extensive. Each ultimate unit of nature, thus conceived, is an event, "with time-duration as well as with its full spatial dimensions."[60] It takes time, in other words, to be actual. Events at the subatomic level may take less than a billionth of a second to occur, but this makes them qualitatively different from matter as traditionally conceived, according to which it can exist in an "instant," meaning a slice of space-time with no duration whatsoever. According to that traditional view, in Whitehead's words, "if material has existed during any period, it has equally been in existence during any portion of that period. In other words, dividing the time does not divide the material."[61] This means that "the lapse of time is an accident, rather than of the essence, of the material. . . . The material is equally itself at an instant of time."[62] In matter thus conceived, there is no internal becoming. The only motion is external motion, or locomotion: the motion of a bit of matter from one place to another.

One side of the mind-body problem can be phrased in terms of the question: How could the locomotion of bits of matter in the brain give rise to the internal motion, or becoming, in our experience? Whitehead's view avoids this question, saying that there is no "nature at an instant," that even the most primitive units of nature have temporal duration, during which internal becoming, analogous to that in our own experience, occurs.

In fact, once temporal duration with its internal becoming has been attributed to all actual entities, it is natural to attribute experience to them, because we have no way to conceive of this internal duration except by analogy with the duration we know in our own experience. Whitehead, accordingly, also referred to actual entities as "occasions of experience," which is a basis for referring to his philosophy as panexperientialism.

In 1977, I coined the term "panexperientialism," saying that it is a better term than "panpsychism" for Whitehead's philosophy, for two reasons. It indicates that the ultimate units of existence are momentary experiences, not enduring things such as psyches. Also, the term "panpsychism" suggests that the ultimate units contain rather high-level mentality, with consciousness.[63] This second problem was, in fact, evidently Whitehead's own reason for eschewing the term.[64] When Charles Hartshorne, who used the term "psychicalism," saw the term used to expound his position, he said: "I do not object to 'panexperientialism' instead of 'psychicalism,' and see advantages in that terminology."[65]

In any case, once the move is made to panpsychism or panexperientialism, the interaction of conscious experience with the neurons in the brain is no longer a complete mystery. As McGinn admitted, if neurons had experience, it would be "easy enough to see how neurons could generate consciousness."[66]

Nondualistic Interactionism

A confusion that runs through most discussions of the mind-body problem is the equation of "interactionism" with "dualism." Cartesian dualism involves two distinct theses—a numerical thesis and an ontological thesis. The numerical thesis simply says that mind and brain are not numerically identical but are two things: The mind is one actuality; the brain is another actuality (or, really, a complexly organized society of billions of actualities).

The ontological thesis of Cartesianism adds that the mind and the brain are two ontologically different kinds of things: The mind is one kind of actuality (a mental one); the brain is another kind (a physical one comprised of insentient particles). A position should be called "dualistic" only if the ontological thesis as well as the numerical thesis are affirmed.

If a position affirms merely the numerical thesis, saying that the words "mind" and "brain" do not refer to the same entity, it should not be called "dualistic," because the word "dualism" inevitably suggests the Cartesian idea that mind and brain are ontologically different types of things, which is the idea that creates the problem of dualistic interaction.

Of course, although the numerical and the ontological theses are distinguishable, they were not separable for Descartes, due to his view of matter, and thereby of the brain, as composed of entities devoid of experience. Given the Cartesian view of matter, the numerical thesis implies the ontological thesis. Because almost all scientists, philosophers, and theologians have retained that early modern view of matter, they perpetuate the assumption that any position that distinguishes (numerically) between mind and brain is ipso facto "dualistic."

For example, philosopher Daniel Dennett's argument that materialism must be true is based on his assumption that the only alternative is dualism, according to which "conscious thoughts and experiences cannot be brain happenings, but must be ... something in addition, made of different stuff."⁶⁷ The transition from the numerical thesis ("something in addition") to the ontological thesis ("made of different stuff") occurred without comment.

Dualists no less than materialists tend to generally assume that the first thesis implies the second. For example, British philosopher John Hick began a chapter on "Mind and Body" thus:

> We have the two concepts of body and mind, and various rival views of the relation between them. According to the ... mind/brain identity theory the two concepts refer to the same entity. This is the monistic option.... [The dualist] option regards body and mind as distinct entities, and indeed entities of basically different kinds.⁶⁸

While making a quick transition from the numerical thesis to the ontological thesis, Hick at least distinguished between them. A few pages later, however, he wrote:

> In rejecting the mind/brain identity, then, we accept mind/brain dualism. We accept, that is to say, that mind is a reality of a different kind from matter.⁶⁹

Here Hick simply equated the two theses.

The importance of this equation, or at least the assumption that the first thesis implies the second, cannot be overestimated. It leads to the conclusion that interaction between mind and brain is unintelligible, because it builds a Catch-22 into the discussion: On the one hand, the very notion of "interaction" implies two distinct things that can causally influence each other. So, if we, with identists, do not (numerically) distinguish the mind from the brain, we cannot affirm interactionism. On the other hand, the assumption that mind and brain are (ontologically) different in kind implies that, although they are (numerically) distinct, interaction between them is inconceivable.

One of the most vicious effects of the modern view of matter is that, by apparently forcing a choice between numerical identism and ontological dualism, it has made a defense of interactionism, and thereby our hardcore commonsense assumptions about the mind-body relation, impossible.

But panexperientialism, by allowing for interactionism without dualism, enables us to make sense of these assumptions:

(1) because the mind is a unified actuality, distinct from the billions of neurons comprising the brain, the unity that characterizes our experience is intelligible;

(2) because the mind is distinct from the brain, and yet not ontologically different in kind from the cells making up the brain, our twofold presupposition about their interaction—that the body influences our conscious experiences and that these experiences in turn influence our bodies—is intelligible;

(3) because the mind at any moment is a full-fledged actuality—as actual as the brain cells and their constituents—we can take at face value our assumption that our apparent decisions, rather than being fully determined by causal forces coming up from the body, are truly "decisions," in which our minds exercise genuine self-determination; and

(4) finally, our conviction that our bodily behavior is significantly guided by these decisions is made intelligible by the idea that the mind, besides being as fully actual as the individual cells comprising the brain, is far more powerful than any of these cells. This idea explains why the mind can exercise a dominating influence over the body, providing that overall coordination that so radically distinguishes the behavior of a living, conscious person from that of a corpse.

It is in terms of this fourfold position that I endorse Dr. Bruce Greyson's view (on page 76) about "the physical brain and the nonphysical mind."[70]

Panexperientialist Emergence

One distinctive feature of panexperientialism of the Whiteheadian-Hartshornean type is its view of emergence. Given the mechanistic view of the ultimate units of nature as vacuous bits of matter, it was impossible to do justice to evolutionary emergence. There was no way to think of the emergence of higher types of actualities out of the organization of lower types. A living cell, for example, could not be thought to have any ontological unity based in a higher type of actual entity in which the distinctively living properties of the cell could inhere.

In the panexperientialist view, by contrast, an actual entity is an occasion of experience, which arises out of the causal influence exercised on it by prior actual occasions, especially those in its immediate environment with which it is contiguous.

In this framework, we can understand evolutionary emergence to involve, at least sometimes, the emergence of higher-order types of actual entities. For example, the atom need not be thought to consist only of its subatomic particles and the relations between them. It can be thought to involve, as well, distinctively atomic occasions of experience, more complex than the electronic, protonic, and neutronic occasions of experience.

In this way, the holistic behavior of the atom—as manifested, for example, in the Pauli exclusion principle (as discussed by philosopher-theologian Ian Barbour)[71]—can be assigned to an inclusive actuality. A molecule, likewise, can be thought to involve, above and beyond atoms, distinctively molecular occasions of experience. Macromolecules (such as DNA and RNA), organelles, prokaryotic cells, and eukaryotic cells can be thought to involve successively higher-level actual entities.

Those who are unfamiliar with microbiology may consider this idea ridiculous, but as pointed out in Chapter 3, microbiologists have shown that bacteria make decisions, which they can do because they have experience and memory. The new microbiology, Lynn Margulis said, dissolves the most difficult part of the mind-body problem.

The Whiteheadian-Hartshornean philosophy does not dictate a priori that higher-level actual occasions emerge at each of these levels: That judgment is to be made on an empirical basis, in terms of whether (say) a water molecule or an organelle shows sufficient unity of response to its environment to merit positing a "regnant" or "dominant" member to account for the unified response. The point is that the panexperientialist philosophy allows us to posit the emergence of such a higher-level member if the evidence warrants it.

A society having such a higher-level member, which gives the society as a whole a unity of experience and response, was called by Charles Hartshorne,[72] as we saw in Chapter 4, a "compound individual," because a higher-level individual has been compounded out of lower-level individuals.

Appendix II

And Hartshorne's idea was praised by Whitehead. In a letter to Hartshorne of 1935, Whitehead said, "Your essay in 'Philosophical Essays' on 'The Compound Individual' is most important, both in its explanation of relationships to the Philosophical Tradition and its development of the new approach as it has gradually emerged in the last 50 years."[73] Although panexperientialism by definition rules out ontological dualism, it allows, unlike materialism, for an organizational duality between aggregational societies and compound individuals. Contrary to Popper, aggregational societies such as telephones do not have experience. This is important enough that I included in my list of core doctrines of process philosophy: *Panexperientialism with organizational duality, according to which all true individuals—as distinct from aggregational societies—have at least some iota of experience and spontaneity (self-determination).*[74]

It would be hard to overestimate the importance of this organizational duality for the Whiteheadian type of panexperientialism. This type, with its distinction between aggregational societies and those with a dominant member, goes back to Leibniz, who, in fact, referred to the mind of the human being (or any other animal with a central nervous system) as the "dominant monad." Leibniz's own version of this doctrine was problematic, of course, insofar as his monads, being windowless, could not really influence each other. But in distinguishing genuine individuals, which act and feel, from aggregational collections of low-grade forms of these individuals, which as such neither act nor feel, he made a crucial conceptual breakthrough. In making this distinction, Hartshorne said, "Leibniz took the greatest single step in the second millennium of philosophy (in East and West) toward a rational analysis of the concept of physical reality."[75]

In the context of this distinction, the existence of "minds" or "souls" in human beings and other animals is not an evolutionarily unprecedented type of emergence, as generally supposed by materialists and dualists alike. Rather, the emergence of a mind out of that complex organization of cells that we call a brain is simply the highest-level example of a type of emergence—including the emergence of eukaryotic cells out of prokaryotic cells—that has been occurring on our planet throughout the evolutionary process.

The human mind seems so unique to us because it is the only emergent actuality that we know from within. However, this emergence is (by hypothesis) only different in degree, not different in kind, from the emergence of living occasions in eukaryotic cells out of macromolecules and organelles. (As Kant realized, the mind seems different in kind from other things because we know the mind from within, other things from without.)

Accordingly, we need not think, contra Searle, that there is nothing in the head but atoms, nor that these atoms are entirely reducible to their subatomic parts. There is the mind. There are the billions of living occasions in the neurons. And there are organellular, macromolecular, and molecular occasions of experience. Also, we need not suppose, contra reductionistic materialists, that our conscious experience somehow emerges magically as a property of insentient atoms, or, with dualists, that our minds have only insentient atoms and subatomic particles with which to interact.

The Relation between Efficient & Final Causation

The Whiteheadian explication of the freedom we all presuppose in practice depends, as we saw in Chapter 4, on the concept of a "compound individual," which has a "dominant" member. It also depends on the understanding of the mind or soul as a personally ordered society of dominant occasions of experience, in which there is a perpetual oscillation between final and efficient causation, that is, between self-determination and causal influence on others.

This language of "perpetual oscillation" seems a better, less confusing, way to describe Whitehead's meaning than his own language of the "perpetual perishing" of subjectivity.[76]

This doctrine explains one of the most difficult of all philosophical problems: that of freedom and determinism or, more precisely, how final and efficient causation are related. The traditional view of the mind, according to which it is simply an enduring mental substance, made it seem as if it must either be totally determined from without, by the efficient causation from the body, or else totally self-determined from within, by its own final causation.

Some philosophers who accepted the second view developed the doctrine of parallelism, according to which mind, while not really interacting with the body, ran along in parallel with it. In the thought of some advocates of parallelism, such as Gottfried Leibniz, the synchronization between our perceptions and decisions, on the one hand, and the events inside and outside of our bodies, on the other, was given a supernatural explanation, in terms of a harmony preordained by God. For other advocates of parallelism, this synchronization was left an unexplained mystery. Either way, however, parallelism was too incredible to attract much of a following. Most philosophers and scientists, accordingly, gravitated toward determinism.

However, if the mind is constituted by a series of momentary experiences, which first exist subjectively and then exist objectively, there is a constant oscillation between final and efficient causation. Each occasion of experience begins by receiving causal influence from prior occasions; it then exercises its own final causation (self-determination in terms of a goal); and then it becomes one of the many efficient causes upon subsequent occasions.

In this way, we can do justice to our hard-core commonsense presuppositions that (1) we are heavily influenced by the causal power of the past, (2) we do, nevertheless, exercise a degree of freedom in each moment, and (3) this free decision influences our bodily actions. Panexperientialism's view of the body then explains how the third of these three presuppositions can be true, namely, that our mental decisions influence our bodily behavior.

Materialists and dualists, as we have seen, have had great difficulty in explaining this influence. This is mainly because they think of the bodily cells as vacuous actualities, which could not conceivably be affected by thoughts, feelings, and decisions.

From this perspective, there is, contrary to John Searle and other materialists, nothing "unscientific" about supposing that the free decisions of the mind cause the molecules in the body to act otherwise than they would if they were in a different environment.

Conclusion

The advocates of both materialism and dualism have typically argued that their own position must be true because the other position is false, while either ignoring panpsychism (panexperientialism) or ruling it out of court. However, neither materialism nor dualism can do justice to our hard-core commonsense assumptions about the reality, the efficacy, and the freedom of our conscious experience. This threefold failure means that dualism and materialism are inadequate not only for morality and religion but also for science, because scientists, in their scientific activities, presuppose all of these beliefs. No worldview can be adequate for science that has no room for the activities of scientists.

Besides being able to endorse our hard-core commonsense ideas, panexperientialism also allows for—within a fully naturalistic worldview—the possibility of life after death. This is the case because it, unlike materialism, says that the mind is distinct from the brain, and because it, unlike dualism, avoids the insoluble problem of understanding interaction between two ontologically different kinds of things.

Endnotes

1. John R. Searle, "Minds and Brains Without Programs," in Colin Blakemore and Susan Greenfield, ed., *Mindwaves: Thoughts on Intelligence, Identity, and Consciousness* (Oxford: Basil Blackwell, 1987), 209–33, at 215.
2. David Ray Griffin, *Unsnarling the World-Knot: Consciousness, Freedom, and the Mind-Body Problem* ([1998] Eugene, OR: Wipf & Stock, 2007), 15–21.
3. Francis Crick, *The Astonishing Hypothesis: The Scientific Search for the Soul* (New York: Simon & Schuster, 1994), 3, 7.
4. Crick, *The Astonishing Hypothesis,* 7, 261.
5. Martin Jay, *Force Fields: Between Intellectual History and Cultural Critique* (London & New York: Routledge, 1993), in a chapter titled "The Debate over Performative Contradiction: Habermas versus the Poststructuralists," 25–37, at 29.
6. John Passmore, *Philosophical Reasoning* (1961; New York: Basic Books, 1969), 60.
7. Alfred North Whitehead, *Process and Reality,* corrected edition, ed. David Ray Griffin and Donald W. Sherburne ([1929] New York:Free Press, 1978), 13.
8. John R. Searle, *Minds, Brains, and Science: The 1984 Reith Lectures* (London: British Broadcasting Corporation, 1984), 8.
9. Searle, *Minds, Brains, and Science,* 13.

10. Searle, *Minds, Brains, and Science*, 86.
11. Searle, *Minds, Brains, and Science*, 94.
12. Searle, *Minds, Brains, and Science*, 97.
13. Searle, *Minds, Brains, and Science*, 97.
14. Searle, *Minds, Brains, and Science*, 95.
15. Searle, *Minds, Brains, and Science*, 97.
16. *Searle, Minds, Brains, and Science*, 87, 92, 95.
17. Searle, *Minds, Brains, and Science*, 89.
18. Searle, *Minds, Brains, and Science*, 92.
19. Searle, *Minds, Brains, and Science*, 7, 15.
20. Searle, *Minds, Brains, and Science*, 8, 13.
21. John R. Searle, *The Rediscovery of the Mind* (Cambridge: MIT Press, 1992), 26–27.
22. Searle, *The Rediscovery of the Mind*, 248.
23. Searle, *The Rediscovery of the Mind*, 247–48.
24. Searle, *The Rediscovery of the Mind*, 13.
25. Searle, *Minds, Brains, and Science*, 92, 93.
26. Searle, *Minds, Brains, and Science*, 88.
27. Searle, *Minds, Brains, and Science*, 93.
28. Searle, *Minds, Brains, and Science*, 98.
29. David Bohm and B. J. Hiley, *The Undivided Universe: An Ontological Interpretation of Quantum Theory* (London & New York: Routledge, 1993).
30. Searle, *Minds, Brains, and Science*, 87.
31. Searle, *The Rediscovery of the Mind*, 111.
32. Searle, *Minds, Brains, and Science*, 94, 98.
33. Hilary Putnam, *Reason and Realism, Philosophy Papers, Vol 3* (Cambridge University Press, 1989), 191.
34. Jaegwon Kim, *Supervenience and Mind: Selected Philosophical Essays* (Cambridge University Press, 1993), 102–07, 348–60, 367.
35. Searle, *The Rediscovery of the Mind*, 8

36. Thomas Nagel, *Mortal Questions* (Cambridge University Press, 1979), 188, 189.
37. Thomas Nagel, *The View from Nowhere* (Oxford Universary Press, 1986), 50.
38. Daniel E. Dennett, *Consciousness Explained* (Boston: Little, Brown & Co., 1991), 458, 459.
39. Searle, *The Rediscovery of the Mind*, 130.
40. John C. Eccles, *How the Self Controls Its Brain* (Berlin: Springer-Verlag, 1994), 22.
41. Karl R. Popper, *Of Clocks and Clouds: An Approach to the Problem of Rationality and the Freedom of Man, Issue 2* (Washington University Press, 1966), 15.
42. Karl R. Popper and John C. Eccles, *The Self and Its Brain: An Argument for Interactionism* (Heidelberg: Springer-Verlag, 1977), 37.
43. Popper and Eccles, *The Self and Its Brain*, 494–95.
44. Popper and Eccles, *The Self and Its Brain*, 16–17, 494–95.
45. Geoffrey Madell, *Mind and Materialism* (Edinburgh: The University Press, 1988), Preface.
46. Madell, *Mind and Materialism*, 2.
47. Madell, *Mind and Materialism*, 140.
48. Madell, *Mind and Materialism*, 140–41.
49. Madell, *Mind and Materialism*, 9.
50. Madell, *Mind and Materialism*, 135.
51. Madell, *Mind and Materialism*, 9.
52. Madell, *Mind and Materialism*, 3.
53. Colin McGinn, *The Problem of Consciousness: Essays Toward a Resolution* (Oxford: Basil Blackwell, 1991, 2n
54. McGinn, *The Problem of Consciousness*, 34.
55. Popper and Eccles, *The Self and Its Brain*, 69, 517.
56. Christof Koch, *The Feeling of Life Itself: Why Consciousness is Widespread but Can't Be Computed* (Cambridge, MA: MIT Press, 2019).
57. Immanuel Kant, *Critique of Pure Reason,* trans. Norman Kemp

Smith (New York: St. Martin's, 1965), 381 (B 428).

58. Pete A. Y. Gunter, "Henri Bergson," in David Ray Griffin et al., *Founders of Constructive Postmodern Philosophy: Peirce, James, Bergson, Whitehead, and Hartshorne* (Albany, NY: SUNY, Press: 1993): 133–64, at 137–41.

59. Colin McGinn (1991) raised the same problem, saying that our perception of matter gives us a purely spatial conception of it—a conception that provides no clue as to how consciousness, which we necessarily conceive in nonspatial terms, could arise from it (*The Problem of Consciousness*, 11, 27).

60. Whitehead, *Process and Reality,* 77; *Religion in the Making*, 91.

61. Whitehead, *Science and the Modern World,* 49.

62. Whitehead, *Science and the Modern World,* 50.

63. David Ray Griffin, "Some Whiteheadian Comments on the Discussion," *Mind in Nature: Essays on the Interface of Science and Philosophy* (University Press of America, 1977), 97–100, at 97–98.

64. A. H. Johnson, "Whitehead as Teacher and Philosopher," *Philosophy and Phenomenological Research* 29 (1969):351–76, at 354.

65. Robert Kane and Stephen Phillips, eds., *Hartshorne, Process Philosophy, and Theology* (Albany, NY: SUNY Press, 1989), 181.

66. McGinn, *The Problem of Consciousness*, 28n.

67. Dennett, *Consciousness Explained*, 27.

68. John Hick, *Death and Eternal Life* (San Francisco: Harper, 1976), 112.

69. Hick, *Death and Eternal Life,* 119–20.

70. Bruce Greyson, *After: A Doctor Explores What Near-Death Experiences Reveal about Life and Beyond* (New York: St. Martin's Essentials, 2003), 209.

71. Ian Barbour, *Religion in an Age of Science* (San Francisco: Harper & Row, 1990), 104–05.

72. Charles Hartshorne, "The Compound Individual," in *Philosophical Essays for Alfred North Whitehead,* ed. Otis H. Lee (New York: Longmans Green, 1936), 193–220; reprinted in Charles Hartshorne, *Whitehead's Philosophy: Selected Essays 1935–1970* (University of Nebraska

Press, 1972), 41–61.

73. This letter was published as an appendix in Victor Lowe, *Alfred North Whitehead: The Man and His Work*, Vol. II (Baltimore: The Johns Hopkins Press, 1990).

74. Griffin, *Reenchantment without Supernaturalism: A Process Philosophy of Religion* (Cornell University Press, 2001), 6.

75. Hartshorne, "Physics and Psychics: The Place of Mind in Nature," in *Mind in Nature: Essays on the Interface of Science and Philosophy*, ed. John B. Cobb, Jr., and David Ray Griffin (University Press of America), 89–96, at 95.

76. Yale philosopher William Christian said of a completed occasion that it "has now perished and is no longer actual." Then, pointing out that "the only 'reasons' according to the ontological principle are *actual* entities" (*An Interpretation of Whitehead's Metaphysics* [Yale University Press, 1959], 322), Christian concluded that past occasions, having "perished" and therefore being no longer actual, could not exert efficient causation upon the present. No greater distortion of Whitehead's meaning could be imagined. Whitehead's point is simply that the occasion's *subjectivity*, or *subjective immediacy*, must perish before the occasion can exist as an object for later occasions, because until an occasion's final causation or self-determination is complete, it *is* nothing determinate and therefore could not exert causal influence upon anything else. Whitehead said: "Actual entities 'perpetually perish' subjectively, but are immortal objectively. Actuality in perishing acquires objectivity, while it loses subjective immediacy. It loses the final causation which is its internal principle of unrest, and it acquires efficient causation" (*Process and Reality*, 29). "Perpetual oscillation" between subjectivity and objectivity seems a better way to describe this.

Index

action at a distance, 33, 46
actual entities, 183, 184, 188, 196n76
actual occasions, 46, 139, 184, 188
occasions of experience, 43, 184, 188, 190
ad hoc hypotheses, 134-35
Adler, Julius, 22n1
Alcock, James, 37
Alexander, Eben, 73
Almeder, Robert, 114n11
Altieri, Charles, 167
American Association for the Advancement of Science, 37
American Society for Psychical Research (ASPR), 40, 53, 55
Apostles (Cambridge), 44, 150
Apparitions, 87, 88, 89, 157, 161; an Ian Stevenson case, 93; collective, 91, 158; Hornell Hart on, 93-94; multiple, 90-91, 158; quasi-physical, 93-94; veridical, 89, 92-94; and OBEs, 93-94
Appearances of Jesus understood as veridical apparitions, 94-95
Aristotle, 47
ASPR, 40
assemblage, 47
Augustine, Keith, 18n2

bacteria, 19, 20-22, 25, 27, 139, 188
Baker, Gordon, 49n12
Balfour, Arthur, 31
Balfour, Gerald, 31
Barbour, Ian, 188
Barnes, Luke A., 131, 142n12
Beauregard, Mario, 82
Becker, Carl B., 95n4, 114n11
Bergson, Henri, 28n6, 183
Bering, Jesse, 102
biocentric, 126, 138, 140, 162
Birch, Charles, 28n6
birthmarks & congenital defects, 105, 106, 158, 162
Blacher, Dr. Richard, 70-71
Blackmore, Susan J., 70, 83nn2-3
Blum, Deborah, 48n6, 50n26, 57, 61,

62, 150
Bohm, David, 28n6, 193n29
Borg, Marcus, 95
Bouhamzy, Ibrahim, 103-04
Bové, Paul A., 168n9
Boyle, Robert, 33
brain and mind, 18-20, 27, 35, 47, 70, 75-76, 78, 82-83, 140, 149, 151, 157, 161, 169, 171, 172, 175-79, 181, 184-87, 189, 192
Braude, Stephen E., 60, 92, 103
Broad, C.D. (Charlie Dunbar), 12, 32, 38, 44, 45, 149
Brüntrup, Godehard, 29n7
Buddhist spiritualities, 13, 100
Bultmann, Rudolf, 120

Cadoux, C. J., 95
Cambridge Conversazione Society (Apostles), 44
Campbell, Keith, 49n15
Carroll, Lewis, 171
Carroll, Sean, 130, 131, 138
causation, causal efficacy, 43
Christianity as One True Religion, 34
civilization, 2
Clark, Kimberly
Cobb, John B. Jr., 119
Collins, Robin, 141n11
compound individuals, 22, 26
commonsense beliefs: hard-core, 169-70; soft-core, 170.
Conley, Michael, 89
Cook, Emily Williams, 85n27
Cooper, Irving Steiger, 159
Cooper, Sharon, 86n44
Corey, Michael, 142n11
Crick, Francis, 170-71

Darwin, Charles, 125
Darwinism, 125
Davies, Paul, 126, 127, 131, 134
Dawkins, Richard, 21
death as a problem, iin1, 6-10

death of Earth, 2-3
Dennett, Daniel, 178, 185-86
Descartes, René; Cartesian, 12, 19, 20, 21, 27, 33, 34, 148, 165, 178, 180, 185
dowser, 40
Dowsers, American Society of, 40-41
dualism, ii, 3, 18, 19, 21, 35, 120, 165, 178-82
Ducasse, C.J., 61
Duran, Jane, 38-39

Eastland, Susan, 110
Eldredge, Niles, 21
electromagnetism, 126, 127
Elewar, Imad, 103-04
Ellis, George, 131-32
empiricism, 35, 36; sensate, 35; radical, 39, 41, 42, 150, 156, 161
epiphenomenalism, 35, 177, 179
epistemology, 35, 41, 156, 166
epochal theory of time, 43
extrasensory perception (ESP), 32, 34, 35, 36, 41, 42, 53, 58, 59, 64, 82, 157
eukaryotic cells, eukaryotes, 21, 22, 26, 139, 189, 190
extinction, 1-2, 11, 155

Fenner, Frank, 2
57-year-old man, 79-80
Ferré, Frederick, 167
fine-tuning, ii, 4, 126; simplest explanation for, 126
Flew, Antony, 37, 38, 39, 129, 136
44-year-old man, 80-81

Gardner, Martin, 49n19
Gauld, Alan, 48n1
George, William, 104-106
Gladstone, William, 31
global warming, 155
God (deity, divine creator, divine reality, Holy Reality), ii, 5, 7, 8, 9-13, 17, 33, 130, 132, 133, 134,

135, 136, 137-38, 140, 141, 159, 160
gravity, 126, 127
Green New Deal, 156
Greene, Brian, 132
Greene, Rosalind, 149
Greyson, Dr. Bruce, 74-76
Grim, Patrick, 49n16
Grossman, Neal, 82
Gunter, Pete, 183
Gupta, Gopal, 108
Gurney, Edward, 87, 88, 147, 151

Hartshorne, Charles, 6, 9, 10, 11, 12, 13, 22, 25, 26, 27, 45, 120, 136, 150, 155, 160, 161, 182, 188, 189; on psychicalism and panexperientialism, 184-85
Harvard University, 6, 8, 42, 43, 45, 54, 82, 94, 126, 177
Hawking, Stephen, 127-28, 130, 131, 138
Hebb, Donald, 38, 39
Heidegger, Martin, 1, 167
Helender, Samuel, 107
Henderson, Lawrence Joseph, 126, 138
Hick, John, 186
Hindu spiritualities, 13
Hodgson, Richard, 55-56, 59, 63, 151-52
Holden, Janice Miner, 74
Holly, 74-75
hope, 2, 5, 8, 17, 148, 155, 159
Hoyle, Fred, 128-29, 136
Hume, David, 35, 42-43
Hyman, Ray, 36-37

identism, 35, 186
inflation, 133-34
insensate matter, 21
IPCC, 2

James, William, i, 3, 4, 25, 26, 28n6, 32, 34, 36, 38-41

Jaskolla, Ludwig, 29n7
Jesus, 34, 36, 94-95, 160
Johnson, A. H., 52n68
Jones, Judith A., 152n
Kant, Immanuel, 7, 9, 12, 136, 183, 190

karma, 101, 159
Keen, Montague, 68n37
Kelly, Edward F., i, 46-47
Knapp, Krister Dylan, 40, 55, 61, 150-51
Kolbert, Elizabeth, 1-2
Koch, Christof, 182
Kuhlmann-Wilsdorf, Doris, 102
Kurtz, Paul, 37

Lake, Kirsopp, 94
Lamont, Corliss, 17-18, 117, 147, 149, 156, 161
Lancet, The, 80
LaSala, Dr. Anthony, 77
late modern worldview, 3, 36, 47, 172
Laudan, Rachel, 49n16
Leibniz, Wilhelm Gottfried, 28n6, 47, 189, 190
Leininger, James, 110-12, 159
Lennox, John, 128
Lichfield, Gideon, 73
life after death, i, ii, 3, 4, 5, 7, 8, 9, 10, 11, 12, 13, 14, & passim
Light, Malcolm, 2
line of demarcation, 36
Locke, John, 35
Lotze, Hermann, 26, 28n6
Lommel, Dr. Pim van, 80-81
Lowe, Victor, 14n5, 44, 45, 52n57, 148, 196n73

MacGregor, Geddes, 100, 106, 107, 113, 159
magical philosophies, 33
Margulis, Lynn, 21-22, 25, 26, 161, 188
Martin, Michael, 18n2

Ma Tin Aung Myo, 103, 108-09
materialism, iin1, 3, 17, 18, 19, 35, 101, 166, 170-77, 178, 180-81, 182, 185, 189, 191-92
Maria, 76-77
Matson, Floyd, 166
Mayer, Elizabeth Lloyd, 40
McDermott, Robert, 48n5, 66n2, 153n22
McGinn, Colin, 19-20, 21, 182, 185
McPherson, Guy R., 2
McTaggart, J. M.E., 149
mechanism, 33-35, 37-39, 140, 156, 161, 166, 175, 187
memory, 6, 20, 43, 119, 183, 188
Mercier, Cardinal, 100
Mersenne, Marin, 33, 34, 49n11
microbial cells, 21, 161
microbiology, 3, 19, 20, 22, 188
mind-body dualism, ii, 18, 35
mind-body (soul-body) problem, ii, 3, 18, 19-22, 25, 27, 28, 33, 34
mind-body relation, 13, 18, 19, 21, 72
Mind in Nature, 28n6, 29n11
miracles, 33, 34, 35, 94, 130, 136, 138
modern worldview, 18; first version, 33-35; second version, 35-36; late, 3, 36, 47, 172
Moody, Dr. Raymond, 70, 75
multiverse hypothesis, 129, 130-31; critiques of, 131-36
Myers, Frederic, 47, 61-66, 88, 151, 157

Nagel, Thomas, 22, 27, 137, 138, 177, 178
naturalism, 22, 27, 33, 35-36, 118, 122, 137, 166
near-death experiences (NDEs), 69, 72, 73, 74, 75, 76, 79, 80, 81, 82
near-death out-of-body experiences (ND OBEs), 69, 70, 71, 72-74, 76, 78, 79, 160, 161; mundane phase of, 69, 70, 72, 74, 77; transcendental phase of, 69, 72, 77, 81; extrasomatic interpretation of, 70; intrasomatic interpretation of, 70; of the blind, 80-81, 85-86n45
neo-Darwinism, 27
neurons, 19-20, 21, 22, 171, 177, 185, 187, 190
New York Times, 8
Newton, Isaac, 33
Niebuhr, Reinhold, 120
Nielsen, Kai, 147
nihilism, 2, 7
nondualistic interactionism, 185-87
non-sensory perception, 43, 156, 161

Occam's Razor, 131
Ogden, Schubert M., 122n7
organelles, 25, 26, 188, 190
omnipotence, iin1, 2, 3, 17, 18, 34, 135, 138, 139, 140, 155, 163n13
objective immortality, 9-10, 11
out-of-body experiences (OBEs), 69-86, 93-94, 157, 160, 161
Origen, 100

Pagels, Elaine, 132
Pagels, Heinz, 132
Paley, William, 125
pantheism, 127, 136
panentheism, 4, 135-41
panexperientialism, panpsychism, 3, 19, 22, 25-28, 169-96; and temporality, 182-85
parapsychology, 36-39, 101
Parapsychological Association, 37
Parnia, Dr. Sam, 79-80
Pauli exclusion principle, 188
Peirce, Charles, 28n6, 139
Penzias, Arno, 130
perceptive experience, 21
perception in the mode of causal efficacy, 42-43, 156, 161
perception in the mode of presentational immediacy, 42
perception in the mode of symbolic reference, 43

Index

Perry, Ralph Barton, 39, 45
physical objects, 43, 93
physical prehensions: pure and hybrid, 46
Pinker, Steven, 82
Plato, 12, 47, 140, 148
Platonic Renaissance, 33
Polkinghorne, John, 131
Popper, Karl, 179, 182, 189
postmodern, 3, 19, 48, 22n1, 49n10, 159, 165-67
Price, George, 37, 39
prokaryotic cells, prokaryotes, 21, 22, 25, 26, 188, 189
pseudoscience, 36, 37
psychical research, i, 3, 4, 12, 31, 32, 34, 35, 36, 38-41; Whitehead and, 41, 44, 45-48
purgatory, 113

quantum physics, 166
Quine, Willard Van, 42

Randall, John Herman, Jr., 166
Rees, Martin, 127
Reeves, Tate, 156
relativity physics, 166
Rensch, Bernard, 28n6
reincarnation, 99-116
resurrection of the soul, 120-22
Reynolds, Pam, 78-79
Richardson, Robert D., 40, 57
Richet, Charles, 31
Ring, Kenneth, 72
Ruskin, John, 31
Ryan, Thomas, 100

Sabom, Dr. Michael, 79
Saltmarsh, H. F., 68n49
Santayana, George, 42
Sartre, Jean-Paul, 9
Schiller, F.C.S., 151
Schilling, Harold, 166
Schopenhauer, Arthur, 99
science-based cosmology, philosophy, 18, 35
scientific worldview, 35
Searle, John, 169-70, 172-77
sensate empiricism, 35
sensory perception, 42
Shapiro, James, 20
Sharp, Kimberly Clark, 84n24
Sherburne, Donald W., 14n1
sensationism (sensationist doctrine of perception), 34, 35, 36, 41-43
Sidgwick, Eleanor (Nora), 65, 88
Sidgwick, Henry, 31-32, 40, 44, 151
Smolin, Lee, 131
Society for Psychical Research (SPR), 31, 32, 40, 41, 44, 47, 53, 56, 58, 61, 65
Spetzler, Dr. Robert, 78
St. Paul, 94, 95
Stephen, Leslie, 31
Stevenson, Ian, 88-89, 91, 93, 101-07, 110, 115n24
Steinhardt, Paul, 131
Stenger, Victor, 142n12
Strawson, Galen, 27-28
Strawson, Peter F., 27
Streeter, B.H., 94-95
strong nuclear force, 126-27
subjective immortality, 13
Sullivan, Al, 77-78
supernaturalism, 18, 33, 34, 35
super-psi, 74
symbiogenesis, 21
symbolism, 118, 120
Swinburne, Richard, 34

Takata, Dr. Hiroyashi, 77
Tarner Lectures, 45
telepathy, 32, 34, 38, 39, 43; Whitehead on, 45-48
Tennyson, Alfred, 31
Tertullian, 122
theodicy, 14
Thielicke, Helmut, 99
thing in itself, 26, 183
time, 43, 183, 184; epochal theory of, 43

Titchener, Edward, 32
Tso, Wung-Wai, 22n3
Tucker, Jim B., 101, 110
Tyrrell, George, 88

ultimate justice, 7, 11
ultimate meaning, 6-7, 10, 11
Umipeg, Vicki, 81
Unger, Roberto Mangabeira, 132

vacuous actualities, 140
Valarino, Evelyn Elsaesser, 84n11
veridical, 103
veridical apparitions, 88
veridical ND OBEs
veridical OBEs, 72, 83
veridical perceptions, 72
Verrall, Helen, 62, 64
Verrall, Margaret, 62-64
Viney, Donald, 13

Waddington, C. H., 28n6
weak nuclear force, 127
Westfall, Richard J., 48n8
Wheeler, John Archibald, 37, 49
Whitehead, Alfred North, 3, 4, 8, 9-10, 11, 12, 25-26, 27
Whitehead, Evelyn, 148
Whiteheadian-Hartshornean philosophy, 188
Whitehead's Gifford Lectures, 149
(Whiteheadian) process philosophy and theology, 5, 9, 10, 11, 14
wholeness, 8-9, 11
Withnail, Adam, 85n40.
Wollersheim, Dexter, 2
Wright, Sewall, 28n6

www.ingramcontent.com/pod-product-compliance
Lightning Source LLC
Chambersburg PA
CBHW072006110526
44592CB00012B/1221